PSYCHOLOGY OF WOMEN

GARLAND REFERENCE LIBRARY
OF SOCIAL SCIENCE
(VOL. 397)

PSYCHOLOGY OF WOMEN
Resources for a Core Curriculum

edited by
Sharon Golub
Rita Jackaway Freedman

Contributors
Ronda Carpenter
Roanoke College

Rita Jackaway Freedman
College of New Rochelle

Sharon Golub
College of New Rochelle

Beatrice Krauss
College of New Rochelle

Kathryn Quina
University of Rhode Island

Nancy Felipe Russo
Arizona State University

Garland Publishing, Inc. • New York & London
1987

Library of Congress Cataloging-in-Publication Data

The Psychology of women.

(Garland reference library of social science ;
vol. 397)
Outgrowth of a report by the Task Force on
Teaching the Psychology of Women, Division on the
Psychology of Women, American Psychological Association.
Bibliography: p.
1. Women—Psychology—Outlines, syllabi, etc.
2. Women—Psychology—Study and teaching—Audio-
visual aids. 3. Women—Psychology—Bibliography.
I. Golub, Sharon. II. Freedman, Rita Jackaway.
III. American Psychological Association. Task Force
on Teaching the Psychology of Women. IV. Series.
V. Series: Garland reference library of social science ;
v. 397. [DNLM: 1. Teaching Materials—bibliography.
2. Women—psychology—bibliography. Z 7961 P974]
HQ1206.P7695 1987   016.1556'33   87-14949
ISBN 0-8240-8486-1 (alk. paper)

Cover design by Alison Lew

Printed on acid-free, 250-year-life paper
Manufactured in the United States of America

To our colleagues and students who want to know more about the Psychology of Women.

CONTENTS

PREFACE

A Task Force on Teaching the Psychology of Women was created by the Division on the Psychology of Women of the American Psychological Association. Six psychologists who are active in Division 35 and who were teaching courses in the psychology of gender began to think about how they could help other psychology professors introduce the content and excitement found in the psychology of women course into the traditional undergraduate curriculum.

This book is an outgrowth of that Task Force Report. It is designed for psychology instructors who appreciate the importance of new research on gender issues and who want to up-date their courses to more accurately reflect this research. In addition it will help those who wish to go beyond the mere presentation of facts by providing effective learning experience which fosters personal growth.

Resource chapters are provided for the following courses: Abnormal Psychology, Adolescent Psychology, Child Psychology, Developmental Psychology, Educational Psychology, Experimental Psychology, Human Sexuality, History of Psychology, Learning and Motivation, Social Psychology, and Statistics. These eleven courses were selected because they often comprise the core curriculum found in psychology departments across the country, and are frequently required for psychology majors. They also reflect the areas of expertise which members of the task force brought to this project.

Each chapter is organized into three sections.

Part I: Discussion Topics and Questions. These are followed by numbers indicating the appropriate reference cross-listed in the comprehensive reference section at the end of the book.

Part II: Exercises and Activities. Some of these may be done in class while others are more suitable as homework assignments.

Part III: Media. Films, film strips, and videotapes are provided along with a brief description and source information.

We have not employed a formal procedure for deciding which materials should be included or excluded from these resources. The suggested topics, questions, and references are neither comprehensive nor exhaustive of the extensive material that is available. Rather they were selected to provide samples and examples of what we have found to be useful in our own classrooms. As is true of most disciplines, the psychology of women is a rapidly growing and changing field. Due to publication lag, there will no doubt be newly revised texts and more current references that should be sought by those who use this book.

The goal is not to have instructors rewrite their syllabi and totally restructure their courses. Rather, the material offered here is meant to serve as a supplementary instructor's manual from which faculty can pick and choose what is most relevant to their courses and to their teaching styles. We hope that this book will make it relatively easy for those who teach undergraduate psychology courses to integrate material from the psychology of women into the core courses and thereby enhance the entire curriculum.

ACKNOWLEDGMENTS

Many thanks are due to members of the Executive Board of Division 35, the Division of the Psychology of Women of the American Psychological Association, for their consistent encouragement of this project. We are especially grateful to Mary Roth Walsh whose kind words and enthusiasm for this book have energized and spurred us along.

INTRODUCTION

In recent years there have been many changes in the life experiences of women and men and in cultural attitudes about what constitutes gender appropriate behavior. Women's studies courses have contributed to these changes by showing that women are worth studying, and by questioning traditional approaches to the presentation of liberal arts subject matter. Psychology of women courses have proliferated along with women's studies courses in other disciplines and they are now found on hundreds of campuses throughout the United States.

However, the goal of women's studies has always been to serve as a catalyst, to aid in transforming traditional academic disciplines so that they more accurately reflect the contributions and experiences of women. It was a belief of this task force that much of the new psychological material relating to women, as well as new approaches to conventional topics, belongs in the traditional psychology courses. For example, a logical place to examine sex role socialization is in developmental psychology courses; the study of gender as related to power should be discussed in social psychology; and courses in experimental psychology and statistics would be the natural places to challenge methodological issues that may have distorted what we know about women. Psychology of women courses with experienced faculty, excellent texts, rich curricula, and other ancillary teaching materials are now available to serve as resources.

Evolution of The Psychology of Women

In the early 1970s, a small group of female psychologists began to take a critical look at the field of psychology from a feminist perspective. They became increasingly aware of some serious problems that reflected an underlying androcentric bias. Theories often rested on the basic assumption that male experience was normative, and that women's behavior should be either identical to that norm, or considered as deviant from it. Females were studied less frequently and sometimes specifically omitted from samples so as not to "contaminate" the data.

xiii

Stereotypes of feminine behavior were assumed to represent the experience of all females and "healthy" feminine adjustment was defined as conformity to the stereotype. Biological explanations for gender differences were readily accepted whereas social factors and social context were frequently ignored. These are some of the criticisms that have been directed at mainstream psychology by feminist psychologists over the past fifteen years. These are the problems that the psychology of women has tried to address (Kahn & Jean, 1983).

As is true of other academic disciplines, psychology has historically reflected the biases prevalent in the general culture. For instance, early research on the smaller brain capacities of females illustrates how psychologists contributed to the "scientific" documentation of the inferiority of women; this research was subsequently used to justify their social subordination. Denmark (1980) points out that myths function as if they were truths and biases serve as self-fulfilling prophecies. She adds that the process of challenging myths about women requires "a willingness to question the assumptions and stereotypes that form the ideological basis of our social system."

In 1973, a petition signed by 800 members was accepted by the American Psychological Association, thereby establishing the psychology of women as a separate division. At the same time, research about women proliferated and prompted the development of new journals such as *Sex Roles* in 1975 and *Psychology of Women Quarterly*, a publication of the new Division 35. Other journals began to devote more space to articles on women's issues. Growing acceptance of the psychology of women as a legitimate field is evidenced by a steady increase in the number of courses focusing on women's issues. A 1972 survey found thirty-two departments that offered such courses. In contrast a 1985 survey of 896 four year colleges in the U. S. with separate psychology departments found 209 (23%) which listed at least one undergraduate course in this field (Walsh, 1986b).

Other surveys confirm that about one-fourth of the psychology departments currently have an undergraduate course on women. The vast majority of schools must therefore rely on other courses to cover the material relevant to women's issues. To what extent such courses are successfully mainstreaming the psychology of women course content is not known. An analysis of introductory course textbooks that were published between 1979-1982 found the treatment of women's issues to be uneven and often added haphazardly as an afterthought (Denmark, 1983).

Although overt sexism in psychology texts and films has been greatly reduced in the past decade, problems remain. Critical examination of such terms as "stages of man" or "masculinity complex" are still needed to sensitize students to the way that language both reflects and creates stereotypic concepts. Likewise, films still need to be critically examined for the portrayal of stereotypic roles, for the use of "cheesecake" (such as in irrelevant beach scenes), and for the authoritative male voice over.

Decisions of inclusion and exclusion are constantly being made by publishers and faculty faced with space and time constraints. There is a natural tendency to spend class time on traditional topics, partly because we are already familiar with the wealth of data that exists in these areas. A professor may devote half an hour to Sheldon's theory of body types and only a few minutes to sex differences in body image because the former seems more accessible to scientific study. However, this differential emphasis may no longer reflect the relative importance of the topic within the field or to the subject.

Goals of The Psychology of Women

The psychology of women has demonstrated that basic theoretical issues can be viewed from a new perspective. The heredity-environment controversy or the question of mind-body integration, for example, can be discussed in terms of "anatomy is destiny" or "homosexuality is unnatural." The extent to which gender and sex are viewed as biological or social variables is part of the broader question of how nature and nurture interact.

An important methodological issue relevant to all psychology courses is the use of gender as an experimental variable. The designations "male" or "female" are often used to discriminate sets of behaviors or characteristics presumed *a priori* to be correlated with maleness or femaleness. Direct observation of the correlates themselves, regardless of whether they occur in males or females, is often more appropriate and leads to different interpretations of results (Freedman, Golub, & Krauss, 1982).

The psychology of women recognizes the authenticity of subjective experience and of female experience in particular. Learning can begin either with data or with experience. The data can be checked out against personal experience, or real life situations can lead to the exploration of new issues. Either approach is valid and both treat the subjective as authentic. Some of the issues in the psychology of women which focus on the everyday problems that women encounter include:

1. Understanding how the body works and who is to control it.

2. Exploring sexual needs and challenging women's role as sex object.

3. Learning to express emotions, those of power as well as vulnerability.

4. Fostering human development and providing for the needs of people of all ages.

5. Assuring equal rights and freedom from gender stereotyping.

Women's studies courses encourage discussion of taboo subjects such as incest, menstruation, and homophobia. Dialogue on these emotionally charged subjects can lead to a sense of relief when students realize that others share their concerns. The use of guided fantasy, classroom simulations, assertiveness training, and role playing exercises are common in psychology of women classes. These foster effective learning and personal growth that is rarely evoked through discourse alone.

The psychology of women is concerned with implementing behavioral change and social reform. A crucial question is: What happens when students leave the classroom at the end of the semester? Do they understand themselves better, feel better about themselves and better about the women in their lives? Do they interact differently with friends, with family members, and with authority figures?

Why Mainstream?

By incorporating a feminist perspective into the psychology core curriculum more students can be reached, including males who are unlikely to take psychology of women courses. Moreover, courses in educational, developmental, or social psychology are frequently required as preprofessional training for nurses, teachers, and business majors who will need an awareness of sex stereotyping in order to function sensitively in their professional work. Courses in experimental psychology and statistics are often required for psychology majors who will then emerge with the skills necessary to question false assumptions about gender. Hence, by incorporating some of the issues generally covered in psychology of women classes into other psychology courses, students will be exposed to male faculty presenting this material, thus lending validity to these issues.

Another goal of mainstreaming is a change in the classroom climate and the development of new teaching styles that reflect a feminist perspective. The aim is to create an equalization of power in the classroom, a climate of trust where students can share ideas and experiences. The Association of American Colleges has developed guidelines for evaluating the quality of educational opportunities available in the classroom and the institutional climate for women as well. The guidelines incorporate recent research on sex differences in verbal and non-verbal behavior and recommendations for administrators, teachers, and women students are offered. Again, the goal is to eliminate the everyday inequities that may occur on a college campus and to create an environment that fosters the full development of all students, women and men (Hall & Sandler, 1982)

Female psychologists experience special problems regarding graduate school admission, employment, tenure, promotion, and equal pay. Undergraduate majors need to become realistically concerned about these problems. Those who are aware of such organizations as the American Psychological Association Division 35 and the Association for Women in Psychology are more likely to become active participants at some point in their careers.

Clearly there is a psychology of women. This book demonstrates the wealth of information about women's lives that is now available. There is theory, research, and a body of knowledge that is mushrooming as more and more psychologists choose to study the experiences of women. The past androcentric bias of psychology has been challenged. To be up-to-date, psychology courses should now incorporate subjects that comprise the psychology of women. These include, for example, information about sex roles and gender differences; biological influences on women's behavior such as the menstrual cycle, pregnancy, and lactation; the significance of physical attractiveness, female sexuality; women and work; mental health issues; and the experiences of minority women.

In taking as its charge the mainstreaming of the psychology of women, this task force set out to develop a resource volume that could be used to introduce psychology of women content and methodology into the more traditionally taught core curriculum courses. We are not suggesting that mainstreaming replace separate courses on women's issues. On the contrary, we see mainstreaming as a natural outgrowth of the recognition of this field, and a process that should not reduce but rather enhance the further development of such courses.

Those instructors whose background in the psychology of women is limited might begin by looking at the popular psychology of women texts and journals listed at the end of this introduction. These offer extensive bibliographies which provide additional support material.

Can the academic community be motivated to mainstream the psychology of women? We are cautiously optimistic. Psychology of women courses have already brought about many changes. Students recognize and question sexist assumptions; they are selecting courses which examine women's experiences. Textbook content and language has changed in response to demands from educators. More women are entering departments of psychology and are raising consciousness in their classes. If these resource papers serve as an additional impetus for change, they will have met our hopes and expectations.

BASIC PSYCHOLOGY OF WOMEN TEXTS AND JOURNALS

Bernard, J. (1981). *The female world.* New York: The Free Press.

Dilling, C., & Claster, B. (Eds.) (1985). *Female psychology: A partially annotated bibliography.* New York City Coalition for Women's Mental Health. 320 West 86 St., New York, NY 10024

Frieze, I. H., Parsons, J. E., Johnson, P. B., Ruble, D. N., & Zellman, G. L. (1978). *Women and sex roles: A social psychological perspective.* New York: W. W. Norton.

Hyde, J. S. (1985). *Half the human experience.* Lexington, MA: D. C. Heath and Company.

Lott, B. (1981). *Becoming a woman: The socialization of gender.* Springfield, IL: Charles Thomas.

Maccoby, E., & Jacklin, C. M. (1974). *The psychology of sex differences.* Stanford, CA: Stanford University Press.

Matlin, M. (1987). *Psychology of women.* New York: Holt, Rinehart and Winston.

O'Leary, V., Unger, R., & Wallston, B. (Eds.) (1985). *Women, gender, and social psychology.* Hillsdale, NJ: Lawrence Erlbaum Associates.

Parsons, J. E. (Ed.) (1980). *The psychology of sex differences and sex roles.* Washington, D.C.: Hemisphere Publishing.

Sargent, A. G. (1985). *Beyond sex roles.* New York: West Publishing Co.

Tavris, C., & Wade, C. (1984). *The longest war: Sex differences in perspective.* San Francisco: Harcourt Brace Jovanovich.

Williams, J. H. (1987). *Psychology of women: Behavior in a biosocial context.* New York: W. W. Norton.

JOURNALS

Feminist Studies
Psychology of Women Quarterly
Resources for Feminist Research
Sex Roles: A Journal of Research
Signs: Journal of Women in Culture and Society
Women & Health
Women & Therapy
Women's Studies Abstracts
Women's Studies International Forum

PSYCHOLOGY OF WOMEN
RESOURCES FOR A CORE CURRICULUM

Abnormal Psychology

I. The effects of inequality on psychological development. Discuss the mental health implications of sex role socialization that teaches boys to develop concepts of self-worth dependent on personal achievements while girls are taught that self-worth is dependent on the approval of others. (87, 291, 441) How do stereotypes interfere with the development of mentally healthy individuals? (86, 87, 139, 261, 386, 441, 445)

II. Reproductive issues. The events connected with reproduction have profound implications for women's mental health, and it is in connection with such events that myths and stereotypes about women are most potent. Contraception, abortion, sterilization, pregnancy, and birth all involve issues with mental health implications. (3, 211, 299, 411) Discuss the conflicts surrounding unwanted and wanted childbearing and how clinicians might help to resolve them. (3, 452) Discuss the implications of myths about menstruation and menopause for mental health. (165)

III. Female sexual dysfunction. Discuss how sexual dysfunction is defined differently for males and females and how the double standard has affected the definition, diagnosis, and treatment of female sexual dysfunction. (80, 299, 412)

IV. Medical model. Consider how the medical model affects the course of diagnosis and treatment (125) and the implications of the use of the medical model in diagnosing women's psychiatric disorders. (360, 445)

V. Women and work. Contrary to stereotypes, women who engage in multiple roles appear to have better mental health than those who do not. Discuss the ways that work can facilitate or impede the development of good mental health for women. (117, 276, 366)

VI.   **Marital roles and mental illness.** Married women, particularly minority women, have higher rates of mental disorder than do married men--a reversal of the sex difference found for other types of marital status. Discuss the reasons for this finding. (14, 87, 174, 175, 291, 395)

What special strengths as well as stresses might be encountered by dual career couples? (5, 395)
Identify sources of stress during divorce that have mental health implications. (276, 448)

VII.   **Sex differences in patterns of mental disorder.** Discuss reasons for the large sex differences in patterns of mental disorder and the use of mental health services. (14, 44, 87, 139, 174, 365)

VIII.   **Mental health services.** In discussing mental health services, it is important to identify the ancillary services, such as child care and battered women's shelters, that are needed if women are to have access to mental health treatment. (87, 305, 335)

IX.   **Diagnosis.** Discuss the impact of cultural differences and stereotyping on the development and application of diagnostic categories. (234, 347, 412)

X.   **Language in therapy.** Discuss the impact of labels on diagnosis.   What does it mean when therapists talk about men being assertive and women being castrating? Note that in the DSM-III sexual overactivity is labelled "Don Juanism" for men and "promiscuity" for women. How   do   the   labels   of   psychoanalytic   theory, particularly, prejudge causation when applied to describe behavior (e.g. penis envy, transference, countertransference)?   (72, 87, 412)   Clients are subject to the beliefs and stereotypes attached to diagnostic labels. (125, 347, 360)

XI.   **Therapist attitudes, stereotypes, and behaviors.** The relationship   between   therapist   attitudes,   sex-role stereotyping, and treatment outcome are complex.

Discuss how sex of therapist, experience of therapist, and sex of client might influence the course of therapy. (48, 66, 67, 68, 86, 87, 125, 138, 224, 226, 231, 378, 385, 423)

XII. **Feminist therapy.** Consider the similarities and differences among feminist therapy, nonsexist therapy, and traditional therapies. Consider how differential power relationships in therapy can affect the therapeutic process and how the different orientations address issues raised by the differential power of therapist and client. (43, 65, 68, 70, 86, 138, 155, 211, 235, 330, 337, 347)

XIII. **Consciousness-raising and assertiveness training.** Discuss the difference between consciousness-raising, assertiveness training, and feminist therapy. (65, 246)

XIV. **Anger and dependency.** Dealing with anger and dependency are critical issues for women in therapy. Compare how different approaches to therapy deal with these issues. (86, 87, 259, 291, 304)

XV. **Ethical issues in therapy.** The ethics code of the American Psychological Association (11) has several sections related to sex bias in therapy, particularly with regard to mandating competency to work with special populations such as women and minorities, and several task forces of the American Psychological Association have developed guidelines for counseling and therapy with women. These guidelines can be read and used as points for discussion in the classroom. They can also be used to assess the adequacy of the textbook's coverage of topics identified in the guidelines. (8, 9, 10, 12)

Sexual intimacy between therapist and client is absolutely prohibited by the ethics code. This prohibition can be communicated and the reasons for its prohibition can be discussed. Who are the sexually involved therapists and how can they be prevented from harming clients? (60, 61, 260)

XVI. **Consumer issues.** Related to ethical issues are other consumer issues, such as finding and choosing a therapist, rights and obligations in the therapy relationship, how to tell whether sexism is interfering with therapy, and how to deal with grievances. (266)

XVII.   **Chronically mentally ill women.** Discuss the implications of the tendency to treat the chronically mentally ill as genderless in the context of male-oriented treatment models. (370, 361, 411) Identify special issues for long term chronically mentally ill women, including those related to their marital family roles. (411) Discuss the reasons that chronically mentally ill women are especially vulnerable to rape and sexual exploitation.

XVIII.   **Psychotropic drugs.** Although there are no major sex differences in the use of illicit psychotropic drugs, when the source of drugs is a physician, the sex difference is substantial. (87, 132, 211, 361, 398) Discuss the reasons for such sex differences and the implications of the use of drugs in treatment for the duration of therapy. (125, 365) Discuss what consumers should ask before accepting a drug prescription. (266)

XIX.   **Alcoholism and alcohol abuse.** Identify sex differences in drinking patterns. Discuss how they reflect sex role norms and expectations. (79, 138, 168, 249, 361)

XX.   **Deinstitutionalization and homeless women.** Discuss the impact of deinstitutionalization on women as both clients and caretakers of the mentally ill. (18, 415) Identify the special issues for homeless women and discuss their mental health implications. (361)

XXI.   **Depression.** Depression is the leading diagnosis for women. Discuss the social and cultural factors that might contribute to this finding, including the congruence of depressive behaviors with female sex role expectations, the socialization of women to repress and deny anger, the contribution of conflicts and dilemmas in work and family roles, stressful life events, and the effect of powerlessness and poverty. (14, 30, 44, 69, 87, 138, 139, 174, 192, 351, 361)

XXII.   **Anxiety and phobias.** How are anxiety and phobias congruent with female gender role expectations? (44, 69, 72, 138, 139)

XXIII. **Eating disorders.** Discuss the social and cultural factors contributing to the substantial sex differences in eating disorders and the predominance of women clients in weight reduction programs. (139, 150, 185, 226, 309, 310, 350)

XXIV. **Rape.** Discuss the myths and stereotypes about rape victims and perpetrators. Examine the cultural factors contributing to the incidence of rape, and identify ways to stop it as preventive mental health strategies. Discuss the factors that increase the risk of mental disorder as a consequence of rape (e.g. being raped by someone who is trusted or having the trauma of the experience compounded by an insensitive justice system). (69, 86, 211, 361, 429)

XXV. **Domestic violence.** Analyze the dynamics of wife-beating and discuss the inadequacy of traditional psychoanalytic theory to explain it. Discuss why beating up one's wife has not traditionally been considered a severe "mental illness." How might the myth of masochism help to perpetuate violence against women? (69, 86, 87, 211, 279, 361, 391, 425, 426, 427, 428)

XXVI. **Incest.** Contrary to Freudian assumptions, the incest taboo is a myth. Discuss the mental health implications of therapists attributing women's reports of incest experiences to fantasies on their part. (86, 197, 211, 361)

XXVII. **Lesbian issues.** Discuss how both homophobia and ignorance about the life experiences of lesbians can affect therapy. Discuss the stress involved in "being closeted," as well as in the coming out process. (123, 138, 247, 281)

XXVIII. **Disabled women.** Just as chronically mentally ill women have been considered genderless, so too have women with physical disabilities. Identify gender differences in the status of persons with disabilities and discuss the implications of those differences for mental health. (134)

XXIX.   **Ethnic minority women.** Discuss the similarities and differences in the roles and status of ethnic minority women. Examine how differences in the lives of ethnic minority women create different needs and issues in the therapeutic process. (31, 68, 79, 87, 124, 225, 308, 341, 361)

XXX.   **Poor women.** The link between poverty and poor mental health is well-documented. The majority of the U. S. population living in poverty is comprised of women and their children. Discuss the potential causes of the link between poverty and mental disorder, particularly depression, for women. (30, 31, 68, 87)

XXXI.   **Older women.** Older women are the fastest growing segment of the U. S. population, and adult women across all ranges have higher rates of distress than their male counterparts. Identify sources of stress for midlife women during the process of aging. How might popular images and stereotypes of older women impede their mental health? Discuss special mental health issues for older women, including widowhood and role loss, and retirement. (192, 263, 286, 354, 361)

EXERCISES AND ACTIVITIES

1. To increase awareness about stereotyping in advertisements for psychotropic drugs, create a collage that depicts the sexual stereotypes found in the advertising of prescription drugs. Collect clippings of newspaper and magazine ads (typically those targeted to psychiatrists, but also those targeted at the general physician) to demonstrate how the media shapes the images of clinical diagnoses of men and women.

2. Have the students keep a log of events that are particularly stressful and upsetting to them. This can be done anonymously. Then collate the events and identify those that are similar and those that are different for males and females. Once the lists are developed for males compared with females, the question can be asked: is it that different events have happened to each sex or is it that both experience similar events, but react differently to them? Depending on the size and diversity of the class, age and ethnic differences can be examined

3. The needs of women alcoholics have been ignored, and historically most of the major research studies of alcoholism had only male subjects. Given gender differences in drinking patterns, examine the textbook for statements that apply to the drinking behavior of males but not females. To illustrate the effects of bias in research and theory when one sex predominates in a diagnosis, in discussing alcoholism, read various passages of the textbook while substituting the pronoun "she" whenever "he" is used. Does the analysis make "common sense" when the male pronoun is used, yet not "ring true" when the female pronoun is substituted? Does the presentation about alcoholics in general really appear only appropriate to males? Does the same thing occur in discussions of diagnoses where females predominate: depression, anxiety, phobias? How much of the

information purporting to describe human behavior appears more applicable to one sex?

4. Aggression is stereotyped as a "male behavior," and women have difficulty in expressing anger. Explore social and cultural aspects of these phenomena and explore whether certain behaviors are considered more aggressive when exhibited by a woman than by a man. Begin with the exercise on defining aggression provided by Benjamin in *Teaching of Psychology, 12,* No. 1, February 1985, 40-42. Adapt the exercise to examine differences in definitions of aggressive behavior for the sexes. Develop two versions of the Aggression Questionnaire items - one purporting to describe behavior by males, and one describing those same behaviors performed by females. When the judgments of the class are collated, is there a consensus in what is defined as aggressive for males? For females? What behaviors are considered aggressive for both sexes? For only one sex? Do the judgments of the male students differ from those of the female students? Are there interaction effects? What implications do the differences have for defining "abnormally" aggressive behavior on the part of men versus women?

5. Explore gender differences in dependency by asking the class how many people they are dependent on and for what. Are the dependencies related to sex role relationships?

6. Interview a female clinician and a male clinician about the belief, values, and assumptions that they bring to therapy. What are the differences? Do they spontaneously mention experiences that reflect their sex role socialization?

7. Visit a mental institution and look for examples of differential treatment of the sexes on the wards. How are the men and women spending their time? Who do they interact with? Do you observe sex-typed behaviors in interactions between male and female patients?

8. Have students look in the *Psychological Abstracts* for one study of mentally ill women which supports traditional stereotypes and one which does not. Have the students critique the studies and discuss them in class.

9. Look at early psychological writings and see how mentally ill women were portrayed. What is different now? What is the same?

10. Explore attitudes towards the elderly. Have students ask other students not in the class to provide three terms or words that come to mind when they hear the term "old person." Do the same with other students for the terms "old man," and "old woman." After the interviews are completed, list all the responses on a black board and have the class determine, by majority vote, which terms are positive, negative, or neutral. Then construct an overall summary table to show which terms were applied to which category. This activity is useful in that it both demonstrates the persistance of negative attitudes and shows students how research can be done.

11. Have the student write on a piece of paper five traits or descriptive nouns which describe a mentally ill person, mentally ill woman, mentally ill man; Black person, Hispanic person, or other minorities, etc. This activity will make the students aware of their particular biases and gives the instructor a chance to correct any misconceptions that might arise.

12. Ask students to write down things about their body that they dislike, if anything. This should be anonymous. Also, ask, each student to write down their sex, whether they believe they are overweight, underweight, or just about right, and if not about right, how many pounds off. Compare and contrast the answers of males and females.

13. Invite a feminist therapist, a behavioral therapist, and a psychodynamic therapist to compare and contrast their approaches before the class.

14. Invite a rape crisis counselor to visit the class and discuss his or her experiences. Note: be aware that when discussing rape, incest, or battering, it is likely that there will be students in the class who have had such experiences. It is important to discuss these issues in a sensitive fashion and to avoid any appearance of blaming the victim.

MEDIA

1. *Abortion: A Different Light.* Videocassette. A variety of women speak about their choice of abortion; clips of clinic violence by and interviews with right-to-life activists. 28 min., color, Beta, VHS or 3/4" videocassettes, Purchase, $75, Rental $15, from Choices, 97-77 Queens Blvd., Forest Hills, NY 11374.

2. *A Case of Suicide.* Film. Stereotyped social behavior is depicted in this film about the suicide of a seventeen year old wife and mother. 30 Min., b/w, $30, NAMH Film Service, 324 N. Fairfax Street, Alexandria, VA 22314.

3. *The Bag Ladies: An Invisible Minority.* Film. The lives of homeless women are examined. Does not include coverage of homeless women with small children. 25 min., color, Dr. Jacqueline Gentry, Room 15CA, NIMH, 5600 Fishers Lane, Rockville, MD 20858.

4. *Being A Prisoner.* Film. Women prisoners discuss their feelings about themselves, their crimes, and serving time. Examines how the justice system punishes women for not fulfilling their traditional roles as wives and mothers while depriving them of alternatives. 28 min., color, $40, Women Make Movies, 257 West 19th Street, New York, NY 10011.

5. *The Best Kept Secret.* Film. Examines a father- daughter incestuous relationship. 10 min., color, $30, Rhinestone Productions, Mobius International, Box 315, Franklin Lakes, NJ 07417.

6. *Bulimia.* Film. Victims of bulimia, including Jane Fonda, discuss their experiences. Examines the causes and treatments of bulimia. 12 min., CRM/McGraw-Hill Films, 674 Via de la Valle, P.O. Box 641, Del Mar, CA 92014.

7. *Childhood Sexual Abuse.* Film. Documentary of the trauma
    experienced by women who were sexually abused during
    childhood. Study guide is included. 45 min., color, $30.50,
    Motorola Teleprograms, Inc., 4825 North Scott St., Suite 23,
    Schiller Park, IL 60176.

8. *Coming to Know.* Film. Two lesbians discuss how their
    identities have developed. 10 min., b/w, $35, Multi Media
    Resource Center, 1525 Franklin St., San Francisco, CA
    94109.

9. *Dyketactics.* Film. Presents lesbian perspective about
    loving women. 4 min., color. $17, Multi Media Resource
    Center, 1525 Franklin St., San Francisco, CA 94109.

10. *Heroes and Strangers.* Film. Examines a young man's and
    woman's attempts to communicate with their fathers. A film
    about men, emotions, and the family. 29 min., color, sale
    price $425, rental $50, New Day Film Co-op, Inc., 22
    Riverview Dr., Wayne, NJ 07470-3191.

11. *I Don't Have to Hide.* Film. Examines some aspects of the
    eating disorders anorexia and bulimia, including societal
    pressures to be thin, achievement of a healthy self-image,
    and the positive effects of sharing fears with others. 28
    min., Fanlight Productions, 47 Halifax Street, Jamaica Plain,
    MA 02130.

12. *It Happens to Us.* Film. Women varying in age, ethnicity,
    and circumstance answer the same questions regarding their
    experience with abortion. The film highlights the
    psychological elements of fear, pain, self-doubt, and
    adaptation. 30 min., color, $30, New Day Films, P.O. Box
    315, Franklin Lakes, NJ 07417.

13. *Joyce At 34.* Film. Examines a woman who faces the
    conflict of work vs. family. 28 min., color, sale price $375,
    rental $40, New Day Films Co-op, Inc., 22 Riverview Dr.,
    Wayne, NJ 07470-3191.

14. *The Last to Know.* Film. Women discuss their problems
    with alcoholism and prescription drug abuse. $75, New Day
    Films, Box 315, Franklin Lakes, NJ 07417.

15. *The Mature Woman.* Film. Presents the myths, stereotypes, and media portrayal of aging adults, which negatively affects the lives of the elderly, particularly older women. 30 min, color, $30, American Personnel and Guidance Association, Film Dept., 1607 New Hampshire Ave., N.W., Washington, D.C. 20009.

16. *Maxine.* Film. A woman in her late forties, dying of cancer, talks dispassionately about her life. Beaten as a child, placed in an orphanage until an early marriage, she cares for her two retarded children, whom she strives to keep out of institutions. 13 min., b/w, $10, The Pennsylvania State University, Audio Visual Services, Special Services Building, University Park, PA 16892.

17. *Miss Baker: Her Loss of Femininity.* Film. When Miss Baker is upset because she has lost her job due to sexual harassment, her therapist sees her as competitive, aggressive, and rejecting of her femininity. 20 min., b/w, $25, Pictura Films, 43 West 16th Street, New York, NY 10011.

18 *Mothers After Divorces.* Film. The experiences of four mothers who are single parents are shown in this film. 20 min., color, $30, Polymorph, 331 Newbury St., Boston, MA 02115.

19. *Mothers Are People.* Film. A widowed black mother explains the problems she encountered seeking a job. 7 min., color, $20, National Film Board of Canada, 1251 Avenue of the Americas, New York, NY 10020.

20. *Mrs. Gray: A Frigid Woman.* Film. This film illustrates how a woman's normal life experiences and reactions to them are interpreted as abnormal by a therapist. Both of the Pictura Films ("Miss Baker" above) depict how sexist therapy misinterprets and denigrates women's experiences. 20 min., b/w, $25, Pictura Films, 43 West 16th Street, New York, NY 10011.

21. *Pins and Needles.* Film. Examines issues faced by a young woman who discovers she has multiple sclerosis. 37 min., color, $20.50, The Pennsylvania State University, Audio Visual Services, Special Services Building, University Park, PA 16892.

22. *Rape Culture.* Film. Issues surrounding rape are explored including: cultural attitudes, images in the media, interviews with Prisoners Against Rape, and with rapists themselves. A good film, but should include discussion of how the film may subtly stereotype rapists as being predominantly black males. 35 min., color, $46, Cambridge Documentary Films, Box 385, Cambridge, MA 02139.

23. *Rethinking Rape.* Film. Examines societal attitudes which lead to and condone acquaintance rape. 26 min., color, $45, Film Distribution Center, 1028 Industry Drive, Seattle, Tukwila, WA 98188.

24. *Sandy and Madeleine's Family.* Film. Documents problems surrounding the divorces and child custody suits of two lesbians. 30 min., $57, Multi Media Resource Center, 1525 Franklin St., San Francisco, CA 94109.

25. *Sometimes I Wonder Who I Am.* Film. Examines the conflicts felt by a young housewife. 5 min., b/w, sale price $95, rental $18, New Day Films Co-op, Inc., 22 Riverview Dr., Wayne, NJ 07470-3191.

26. *Straight Talk About Lesbians.* Film. A good introduction to a controversial topic, this film is both direct and humorous. Women's Educational Media Inc., 47 Cherry Street, Somerville, MA 02144.

27. *Susana.* Film. Demonstrates the problems of a young lesbian as she confronts the disapproval of her parents. 24 min., b/w, $50, Multi Media Resource Center, 1525 Franklin St., San Francisco, CA 94109.

28. *39, Single, and Pregnant.* Film. Portrays the issues surrounding a single woman's decision to have a child because she felt her "time was running out." 18 min., color, $40., Filmakers Library, Inc., 133 East 58th Street, New York, NY 10022.

29. *To Have and To Hold.* Film. Examines the problem of the abuse of women through men's experience of it. Explores the personal and societal attitudes which lead men to do violence to those nearest to them and examines the changes in attitudes that are essential for men to stop their violent behavior. 20 min., color, sale price $395, rental $40, New

Day Films Co-op, Inc., 22 Riverview Dr., Wayne, NJ 07470-3191.

30. *Welcome To Parenthood.* Film. A disillusioned mother, a father who did not want any children, and a couple who share childraising responsibilities discuss caring for their children. 16 min., color, $17.50, The Pennsylvania State University, Audio Visual Services, Special Services Building, University Park, PA 16892.

31. *We Will Not Be Beaten.* Film. About women's relationships with their abusing husbands, their families, their children, and the justice system. 35 min., b/w, $45, Transition House Films, 120 Boylston Street, #708, Boston, MA 02116.

32. *What Shall We Do About Mother?* Film. (Parts one and two.) Examines the emotional and financial problems of the elderly, focusing on the middle class who are "too rich" for government subsidies, but too poor to afford private nursing homes. 49 min., color, $27.50, The Pennsylvania State University, Audio Visual Services, Special Services Building, University Park, PA 16892.

33. *Who Remembers Momma?* Film. Examines the problems faced by middle aged women, who through divorce lose their role as homemaker, and sometimes even their children. 59 min., color, $24, The Pennsylvania State University, Audio Visual Services, Special Services Building, University Park, PA 16892.

34. *Why Men Rape.* Film. Interviews with convicted rapists and authorities on sexual violence. Points out rape is usually an act of rage rather than sexual lust. Also includes discussion on "social rape." 40 min., color, $25.50, The Pennsylvania State University, Audio Visual Services, Special Services Building, University Park, PA 16892.

35. *Why Women Stay.* Videocassette. Battered women discuss barriers to leaving a battering relationship. 30 min., 3/4" cassette, Women Make Movies, 257 W. 19th Street, New York, NY 10011.

36. *Would I Ever Like To Work?*   Film.   A welfare mother with
    seven children describes her desire to work and examines
    the barriers to her doing so.   9 min., color, $20, National
    Film Board of Canada, 1251 Avenue of the Americas, New
    York, NY 10020.

Acknowledgments
Thanks are due to Ria Hermann for her assistance in collecting
and summarizing information about films and activities for this
chapter.

Adolescent Psychology

TOPICS FOR DISCUSSION

I. **Cross cultural comparison of puberty rites.** Contrast taboos and rituals for each sex. Consider sex differences in contemporary rituals such as Bar Mitzvah, sweet sixteen parties, confirmation. (51, 436)

II. **Achievement motivation.** Do sex differences in independence training in childhood and restricted activities in adolescence result in low female achievement expectations? Do adolescent women experience fear of success when competing with men, and do they inhibit their performance to boost male egos? Can a girl afford to beat her boyfriend on the tennis court? Do attribution errors perpetuate low expectations in women? (112, 315, 376, 396)

III. **Adolescent pregnancy.** Whose fault is it? When is motherhood good and when is it bad? Consider cultural pressures for and against parenthood under various conditions. (41)

IV. **Erikson's stage of Identity vs. Role Confusion.** Consider the special problems of young women who face the double bind, wanting both career identity and family identity. Do young women pursue identity through intimacy? (41, 112, 116, 317)

V. **Moral development.** Discuss sex differences in styles of moral reasoning. For example, abstract universals (masculine) vs. immediate personal feelings (feminine). How do young women resolve the moral dilemmas associated with sexual choices, contraception, and abortion, as compared with young men? (156)

VI.   **Puberty.** How are anatomy and destiny related? Consider the different effects of early and late maturation in each sex as related to both biological and social phenomena. (166, 191, 213, 344)

VII.   **The case of the disappearing tomboy.** Why does she fade away and where do all the sissies go? Discuss androgyny as a threatening concept for adolescents. (33, 142, 218)

VIII.   **Schools as socializers.** How is the acquisition of gender part of the hidden curriculum in the American High School? Discuss teacher reaction to aggressive and dependent behavior in the classroom. Consider Title IX and high school athletics; athletic competition and its effects on personality development in boys and girls. (25, 93, 190, 377)

IX.   **Maladjustment in adolescence.** Why is anorexia a "female" problem? Consider anorexia in terms of media influence on beauty standards, and as achievement motivation turned inward. What are the origins of sex differences in depression, delinquency, suicide, and drug abuse? (58, 143, 262, 321, 388)

X.   **Adolescent identification in single parent families.** Describe role modeling in father absent or mother absent homes.

XI.   **Black and Hispanic adolescents.** What are their special problems and how do their gender role experiences differ from white peers? (384)

EXERCISES AND ACTIVITIES

1. Are vocational aspirations of college seniors sex-typed? Survey males and females with the same major; compare expected salary, long term aspirations.

2. Design a puberty rite for menarche that could be feasibly introduced into our culture. Survey seventh grade girls to see if they would try it.

3. Examine content and ads of magazines aimed at adolescent readers. Contrast *Seventeen* with *Popular Mechanics*.

4. Consider adolescent fashions over the past fifty years and bring in pictures. How does fashion reflect gender roles and encourage or inhibit certain forms of behavior? Do current adolescent fashions reflect a trend toward androgyny?

5. Have both a male and a female answer an ad for a "stereotypic" adolescent job, (i.e., babysitter, gas attendant, stockboy). Compare responses of employers to each applicant.

6. Role play various aspects of a dating situation (initiation of contact, choice of activity, payment, touching, plans for future contact). Reverse roles and play the opposite sex.

7. Interview an anorexic, a teenage mother, an adolescent who has had an abortion, a runaway, a prostitute.

8. Keep a behavioral journal during the term noting the times when a stereotyped role was played. Will such roles diminish or increase as the student passes from late adolescence into young adulthood?

9. Interview pairs of adolescents and their parents to assess generational differences in attitudes toward the Equal Rights Amendment, abortion, homosexuality, unwed mothers, virginity.

MEDIA

1. *Am I Normal?* (1980). Film. A humorous situation comedy about the experiences boys go through during puberty. Presents facts about male sexual development while simultaneously raising important issues about masculinity, identity, and peer pressure. 24 min., color, New Day Films, Box 315, Franklin Lakes, NJ 07417.

2. *Anything You Want To Be.* Film. A teenager's humorous collision with sex role stereotypes. A funny/not funny story of a high school girl who gets conflicting verbal and non-verbal messages. Brief but delightful and imaginative. 9 min., b/w, New Day Films, Box 315, Franklin Lakes, NJ 07417.

3. *The Flashettes.* Film. Shows how young urban women can develop, through rigorous sports training, a positive self-identity. Useful in depicting the different role of athletics in the lives of adolescent boys and girls. 20 min., color. New Day Films, Box 315, Franklin Lakes, NJ 07417.

4. *Girls at 12.* (1974). Film. Examines three twelve year olds and the factors that shape their lives and attitudes about being pretty, popular, becoming a woman. 30 min., color, Educational Distribution Center, 39 Chapel Street, Newton, MA. 02160.

5. *Good Girl.* Film. A reenactment of a diary kept by the filmmaker during her thirteenth year. Examines the loneliness and self doubt that underlie the cheerful diary entries. Reflects the confusion of sex role identity during early adolescence. 45 min., color, Filmakers Library, 133 E. 58th Street., New York, NY 10022.

6. *Growing Up Female.* Film. Shows the socialization of the American woman through a look into the lives of six women ages 4 to 35. Examines the role of parents, teachers,

23

guidance counselors, advertising images, pop music, and the institution of marriage. 50 min., b/w, New Day Films, Box 315, Franklin Lakes, NJ 07417.

7.   *It's Her Future.* (1978) Film. Focuses on the importance of vocational training for girls and features interviews with women in non-traditional technical careers.   17 min., Educational Distribution Center, 39 Chapel Street, Newton, MA. 02160.

8.   *Teenage Pregnancy.*   Three filmstrips with cassettes. Explores the reasons for the rise in teenage pregnancies, discusses the medical risks, emotional problems, and difficult decisions that are faced by a young adolescent couple. Focus International Inc., 1776 Broadway, New York, NY 10019.

Child Psychology

TOPICS FOR DISCUSSION

I. **The decision to become a parent.** One of the reasons for studying child development is the anticipation of becoming a parent. In what ways are people influenced by society to want to become parents? Are the pressures different for women and men? (42, 187, 223) The availability of alternative techniques of reproduction (e.g., *in vitro* fertilization) has extended the option of biological parenthood to infertile individuals. For what reasons do people reject them? Are there differences between women and men in their acceptance of the various alternatives? Why or why not? (91)

II. **Prenatal development** Textbooks focus on the potential damage to the fetus if the pregnant woman smokes, drinks alcohol, etc. Discuss pregnancy from the woman's point of view. How does pregnancy change a woman's life? What are the worries and concerns of the pregnant woman? (334, 417)

III. **Birth.** Textbooks focus on birth conditions for the neonate, and some now emphasize nonmedicated delivery as optimal for the infant. Discuss the decisions about how and where to give birth from the woman's perspective. What are the advantages and disadvantages of "natural childbirth" for the mother? Is nonmedicated delivery necessary for the infant to be healthy? Has natural childbirth become a "test of womanhood," producing guilt for those women who receive medication? (16, 244, 255, 417) How were infants delivered in Western societies before women were hospitalized? What are the advantages and disadvantages of hospital delivery? What are the alternatives to hospital delivery? (16, 294, 403)

IV. **On becoming a mother.** Many people assume that a woman
"naturally" knows how to be a mother. Why do some people
believe that women possess a "maternal instinct"? Are there
alternative explanations for women's ability to perform the
tasks of caregiving, or for many men's reluctance to
perform these tasks, especially for infants? (154, 251, 339)
There is currently an emphasis on immediate mother-infant
contact in order to ensure a "natural" bonding of mother to
infant. Is there evidence that attachment of mother to
infant is impeded by short-term separation after birth?
What would be the advantages of rooming-in for the
mother? (90, 298, 339, 340, 403) Breastfeeding is regarded
by many physicians and psychologists as the preferred
method of feeding. What are the advantages and
disadvantages of breastfeeding from the mother's
perspective? (17, 163)

V. **Childrearing.** Textbooks describe various styles of
childrearing and their relationship to child behavior.
Discuss several childrearing issues from the parent's
perspective. What are the differences between the mother's
childrearing role and the father's childrearing role as
children develop from infancy through middle childhood?
(42, 136, 158, 296) What are the advantages and
disadvantages of being a mother who works outside the
home? How does the father's role change when the mother
is employed? How do children of employed mothers differ
cognitively and socially from children of non-employed
mothers? (21, 38, 205, 206, 228)

VI. **Sex differences, sex typing, and sex role development.** Why
do the majority of couples prefer a son first, or prefer a
son if there is to be only one child? What would (or will)
be the consequences of choice through amniocentesis and
abortion? (128, 133, 277, 319) What does the custom of
using the father's surname for all children indicate about
the relative importance of men and women in our society?
How do adults respond to children who are not appropriately
sex typed? How do other children respond? What kinds of
pressures do teachers and peers place on children to
conform to sex-role stereotypes? (221, 254) Can children
be reared without sex roles? What would society be like if
there were no sex roles? (24, 25, 172, 221, 278, 296, 390)

EXERCISES AND ACTIVITIES

1. Use the course content to write about one or more of the following topics. The papers need be no longer than three typewritten pages and can be discussed in small groups. Persisting assumptions about sex roles may be examined in the students' work.

   a) How I plan to rear my son
   b) How I plan to rear my daughter
   c) How I plan to rear my son to be androgynous
   d) How I plan to rear my daughter to be androgynous

2. Students may examine the "Sex Role Development" sections in old editions of child psychology textbooks and compare them to their own textbook. Libraries (or instructors) usually have copies of editions from the 1940s, '50s and '60s. It is instructive to see the changes in opinion across the decades and sexist statements are not difficult to find.

3. Examine several popular books on childrearing and compare the advice therein to the content of the textbook. Of particular interest is the advice on sex typing [e.g. "Education for Manhood and Womanhood" in *Between Parent and Child* (1965) by Hiam Ginott]. This project may be done with an historical perspective or with contemporary books only.

4. Monitor television programs designed for children (e.g. Saturday morning cartoons) and those broadcast during the late afternoon and frequently watched by children (usually re-runs of situation comedies) and analyze the content of sex role stereotyping. Of particular interest would be portrayal of boys vs. girls, men vs. women, and fathers vs. mothers with respect to personality traits, social interaction patterns (e.g. dominance), occupations, and/or aspirations. In addition to the program content, the advertisements can also be analyzed for stereotyped content.

27

5. Conduct a study of attitudes held by peers, using either an interview or questionnaire methodology. Students may work in small groups on different topics, or the entire class may collect data on the same topic. The following are a sample of relevant topics:

    a) Why one does or does not plan to become a parent
    b) Preference for gender of first-born and later-born children
    c) Perception of role of mother in childrearing
    d) Perception of role of father in childrearing
    e) Plans regarding employment after a child is born (self, if female respondent; wife, if male respondent)
    f) Plans regarding sex-typing of children

MEDIA

1. *And Baby Makes Three: Balancing Everyone's Needs.* Film and Videotape. One couple chooses to have wife stop working, the other balances work and parenting. 27 min., Filmakers Library, Inc., 133 East 58th Street, New York, NY 10022.

2. *Girls at 12.* (1974). Film. Documentary. Three 12-year-old girls learn from their sisters, peers, parents and teachers what being a female means. 36 min., Educational Distribution Center, 39 Chapel Street, Newton, MA. 02160.

3. *The Pinks and the Blues.* (1980). Videotape. Describes research on sex-typing from infancy through middle childhood. Presents research by Parke, Serbin, and others, with emphasis on Dr. Jeanne Block's studies. 60 min., NOVA presentation on public television, $31.50, The Pennsylvania State University, Audio Visual Services, Special Services Building, University Park, PA 16892.

4. *Welcome to Parenthood.* (1981). Film and Videotape. Three couples discuss how children change their lives. 16 min., Filmakers Library, Inc., 133 East 58th Street, New York, NY 10022.

Developmental Psychology

TOPICS FOR DISCUSSION

I. **Life span methodology.** Age cohorts are not always stage cohorts, thus age related stages may be quite different for males and females (i.e., the pregnant fourteen year old girl who is going out with a twenty year old may have little in common with her male age cohorts). Why is this an important methodological issue? Sex differences which are statistically significant may or may not be important to the individual because of social factors. For example, male balding becomes important in societies that emphasize youth. (362)

II. **Heredity and environmental interaction.** Infants are often studied to reflect the influence of heredity "free" of environmental factors. What sex differences have been found in infancy? What is the immediate effect of assignment of sex at birth? Discuss differences in treatment of male and female infants. (19, 35, 272, 353, 371)

III. **Technology and gender.** The effect of science on human development and gender roles is of growing importance, as seen in such issues as prenatal sex planning, abortion of "wrong" sex fetuses, transsexual operations, cosmetic surgery. (239, 397)

IV. **Language and gender roles.** How does sexism in language affect children of different ages? Examine the textbook used in the course for the generic "he" or other examples. How are women infantilized by calling them "girls" or "babes"? Examine such terms as tomboy, bachelor, spinster, middle aged, man and wife, ladies, gals and guys. (215, 250)

V.   **Masculine as normative.** In what ways do some of the major developmental theories reflect a bias that the male experience is normative for the human experience?   Freud, Erikson, and Kohlberg are examples that lend themselves to such criticism. (114, 157, 216, 236, 290, 406)

VI.   **Adolescence.** Consider the different effects of early and late maturation in each sex as related to biological and social factors. Is anatomy destiny? (112, 344)

VII.   **Sex stereotyping in the schools.** What part do schools play in perpetuating gender roles? What changes have occurred over the past ten years and what has been the effect of these changes on children's behavior, self-concept, and future expectations? (47, 118, 140, 374)

VIII.   **Parenting.**   Children have different kinds of relationships with their mothers and fathers. How does mothering typically differ from fathering? How does same sex parenting differ from cross sex parenting? (40, 130, 251, 252, 274, 333, 382)

IX.   **Child care.** With mothers in the labor force in large numbers, who is raising the children? What are the myths about the working mother? Are fathers playing a greater role in child care? Does the working mother have more power in the family? (204, 267, 357, 450)

X.   **Gender acquisition.** Trace the acquisition of gender from infancy through adolescence. Contrast the psychoanalytic, behaviorist, and cognitive approaches. How would each of these theories deal with the concept of androgyny? (267, 320, 323, 402)

XI.   **Family violence.** How do such issues as incest, child abuse, and spouse abuse reflect the negative aspects of traditional sex roles? Who commits family violence and who are the victims? (152, 198, 424)

XII.   **Middle and old age.** While some gender differences disappear with age, the lives of women and men over fifty are often quite different. Consider the empty nest syndrome, sexual decline, retirement, widowhood, longevity, in terms of the different experiences and strengths of men and women. (22, 28, 326, 354)

XIII. **Minority and cross-cultural experiences.** The black woman has special problems as a "double" minority person. Compare modern American sex roles with those assigned in other cultures. (327, 438)

EXERCISES AND ACTIVITIES

1. If one has access to an infant, dress it first as a male and then as a female and record the different reactions of people in public places such as a supermarket, cafeteria, dormitory.

2. Do an autobiographical self study. Consider how one has conformed to gender role expectations over the past few years, with respect to appearance, sports, career choice, dating patterns, family expectations, etc. Take the Bem Sex Role Inventory and consider the score in terms of how well it predicts your own behavior.

3. Compare popular child care handbooks as they reflect changes over the past fifty years in gender expectations for children. Examples: Watson, J. B., *Psychological Care of Infant and Child*, 1928; Spock, B., *Baby and Child Care*, 1945, 1957, 1978 (contrast all three).

4. Consider one's own family in terms of sex roles. How is the labor divided? Who makes decisions in what areas? What roles do different siblings play? What expectations do you have for division of labor in your future family?

5. How are gender roles depicted in children's books? Examine books for several age levels looking for themes, appearance of characters, activity level, parental roles. The same can be done for children's television. Watch several hours of cartoons and merely count the number of male and female characters and the number of comments they make.

6. Visit a school and look for examples of sex stereotyping in the classroom. Do children walk through the halls in sex segregated lines, do they play together at recess, do boys and girls play different games? If so, ask them why?

7. Have a panel of working mothers come to class to discuss their experiences with respect to child care. The same can be done for single parents, fathers raising children, blended families.

8. Do a detailed in-depth study of a school age or adolescent child to explore his/her feelings about gender. In what ways does the child conform to traditional stereotypic roles? How does the child feel about her own sex, the opposite sex, the way boys and girls treat each other?

MEDIA

1. *Am I Normal?* (1980). Film. A humorous situation comedy about the experiences boys go through during puberty. Presents facts about male sexual development while simultaneously raising important issues about masculinity, identity and peer pressure. 24 min., color, $40, New Day Films, Box 315, Franklin Lakes, NJ 07417.

2. *Battered Spouses.* Film. Presents the plight of the victim but also explores the many alternatives that are becoming available to battered women today. 28 min., color, Harper and Row Media, 2350 Virginia Ave., Hagerstown, MD 21740.

3. *Chillysmith Farm.* (1981). Film. An unforgettable film raising issues on values, family life, birth, death, and individual responsibility for the aging. Stereotypes are questioned and a satisfying lifestyle is forged. 55 min., color, $80, Filmakers Library, Inc., 133 East 58th Street, New York, NY 10022.

4. *Growing Up Female.* Film. Shows the socialization of the American woman through a look into the lives of six women ages four to thirty-five. Examines the role of parents, teachers, guidance counselors, advertising images, music, and the institution of marriage. 50 min., b/w, New Day Films, Box 315, Franklin Lakes, NJ 07417.

5. *Joyce At 34.* Film. Examines a woman who faces the conflict of work vs. family. 28 min., color, sale price $375, rental $40, New Day Films Co-op, Inc., 22 Riverview Dr., Wayne, NJ 07470-3191.

6. *Men's Lives.* (1974). Film. Examines the prevailing image of masculinity in America, including interviews in which several boys and men discuss their experiences. An Academy Award winning documentary it gives fresh insight

into the male mystique.   43 min., color, New Day Films, Box
315, Franklin Lakes, NJ   07417.

7.   *Nana, Mom and Me.*   Film.   The filmmaker, who is
considering   having   her   first   child,   examines   the
interrelationships between herself, her artist mother, and
her grandmother.   Does not present pat answers but
attempts to find a means to bridge the generations.   47
min., color, New Day Films, Box 315, Franklin Lakes, NJ
07417.

8.   *Sally Garcia and Family.*   Film.   Deals with the issues that
surround the separate demands of children, husband, work,
continuing education, and the need for every individual to
do something for her own satisfaction.   35 min., color,
Educational Distribution Center, 39 Chapel Street, Newton,
MA   02160.

9.   *Sex Role Stereotyping in Schools.*   Film.   A series of three
films which present examples of stereotyping as it occurs in
familiar contexts between teachers and students and among
students alone.   Addresses different categories of behavior
including   physical   activities,   social   and   emotional
experiences, intellectual endeavors, and career preparation.
35 min., University of California, Extension Media Center,
2223 Fulton Street, Berkeley, CA 94720.

Educational Psychology

TOPICS FOR DISCUSSION

I. **Sex differences in ability and achievement.** What are the empirically demonstrated sex differences in ability? When do the differences appear developmentally? (269, 271) Why do the sex differences in ability exist? What is the evidence for differential socialization being responsible for differences in cognition? What is the evidence for a genetic explanation? What is the "male" brain vs. the "female" brain hypothesis? (170, 271, 392) How has the sex difference in achievement in mathematics been explained? What is the status of "math anxiety"? (36, 141, 416)

II. **Handling sex differences.** How should classroom teachers use their knowledge of sex differences to aid their pupils (e.g., should girls receive more instruction in mathematics than in English or should they receive less in math than in English)? How can teachers avoid creating a self-fulfilling prophecy with respect to sex differences in ability and achievement? (181, 303)

III. **Sex role stereotyping in the schools.** How do teachers' stereotypes and expectations influence their treatment of girls as compared to boys in setting standards for performance (e.g., are girls required to write more legibly)? In disciplinary actions (e.g., are boys reprimanded but girls ignored)? In assignments of academic subjects (e.g., do boys write about George Washington while girls write about Betsy Ross)? In allocation of classroom responsibilities (e.g., do girls distribute materials while boys re-arrange furniture)? (26, 39, 50, 171, 237) How do the requirements of elementary school reinforce the traditional female sex role and conflict with the traditional male sex role? Who is "victimized" by this more in the short-run and in the long-run? (26, 39, 303, 369) To what extent are contemporary curricular materials stereotyped? How can a teacher recognize sex role stereotyping in textbooks, etc., and counteract them? (245, 393, 369)

IV. **Careers in Education.** Textbooks discuss teaching as a career but do not present it as a "women's career." Discuss the relative percentages of women and men who are elementary vs. secondary teachers, principals vs. teachers, administrators vs. principals, and the probable reasons for the discrepancies. Such discussion should not be intended to discourage women from becoming teachers or to demean classroom teaching as a profession, rather to encourage women education students to aspire to rise in the education hierarchy.

EXERCISES AND ACTIVITIES

1. Students may examine textbooks and other curricular materials appropriate for the grades they plan to teach and analyze the content for sex role stereotypes.

2. Observe classes in local schools. Focus on sex role stereotyping in one or more classroom visits, observing teacher behavior, classroom materials, and student behavior. At least two students should observe at the same time, and the results should be written and/or discussed in class.

3. Examine the employment pattern in local public schools to determine the extent to which women have become integrated into the top level administrative positions. A comparison of the number of women vs. men who are teaching various subjects (e.g., English vs. mathematics), who are elementary vs. secondary school teachers, who are principals, who are superintendents can be surprising to students who don't believe that discrimination and "women's" vs. "men's" jobs still exist today.

MEDIA

1. *Anything They Want To Be.* (1974). Film. Sex role stereotyping in schools. 12 min., University of California, Extension Media Center, 2223 Fulton Street, Berkeley, CA 94720.

2. *Changing Images: Confronting Career Stereotypes.* (1975). Film. A class of third and fourth graders explore career expectations. 17 min., University of California, Extension Media Center, 2223 Fulton Street, Berkeley, CA 94720.

3. *Happy To Be Me.* (1979). Film. Documentary. Students (K-12) express their attitudes toward sex roles. 25 min., Arthur Mokin Productions, Inc., 17 West 60th Street, New York, NY 10023.

4. *Hey! What About Us?* (1974). Film. Vignettes of sex role stereotyping in physical education and play. 10 min., University of Illinois Film Center, 1325 South Oak Street, Champaign, IL 61820.

5. *I Is For Important.* (1974). Film. Vignettes of sex role stereotyping in emotional expression and social interactions by teachers and peers. 12 min., University of Illinois Film Center, 1325 South Oak Street, Champaign, IL 61820.

Experimental Psychology

TOPICS FOR DISCUSSION

I. **The role of personal-political values in science.** Is science "pure", "objective", "rational", and unbiased? (127, 342) To what extent do personal or political values affect research? (242, 420) How has the research process itself ("the experiment") been affected by personal or political values? (105) Are traditional researchers value-free, and feminist researchers biased? (443) For a delightful historical perspective, see (380).

II. **Gender bias in the scientific process.** Examples of bias can be found throughout the scientific process, in the development of theory, the experimental design, the interpretation of data, and the dissemination of results. (Overviews are found in 145, 179, 214 and 430; while a detailed review is available in 287.) Forms of bias include:

    a) Norming of theory to males (233, 430); specific examples in well known areas are provided by Gilligan in moral development (157); Horner in achievement motivation (208); Hubbard and Lowe and Weisstein in comparative psychology. (212, 439)

    b) Bias in test construction, including male-norming (189); assumptions about masculinity, femininity, and homosexuality (63, 95); and measures more familiar to members of one gender, (119)

    c) Role of subjects own biases and stereotypes in their responses to the research task. (388)

    d) Selection of subjects (179), and generalization from "males" to "all humans." (104, 383) Comparable problems can be found with respect to minority women as subjects of research on women. (6)

    e) Use of inappropriate control groups. (313)

f)   Interpretations of research results when sex differences are observed (88, 179, 271), including attributions to personal, rather than situational variables (119, 146, 336, 378), and assumptions that sex differences have a biological basis. (84, 126, 178) An interesting analysis of subtle bias through the terms used in discussing sex differences and misunderstandings arising from poorly defined use of terms "sex" and "gender" are described in (149, 418).

g)   Emphasis on p values (52), and journal editorial policies of only publishing studies with statistically significant differences (180), overestimate any differences that have been observed (179, 271), including those found by chance alone.

III.   **New perspectives on research.** The view students receive of the research experiment can be greatly expanded, at both ends of the quantitative spectrum.

a)   New methodologies, especially meta-analysis, have introduced the ability to analyze a large body of literature.   This methodology also provides perspective on the relation between statistical and practical significance. Meta-analyses on cognitive abilities (214, 221), mathematics (348), and social conformity (119), can be used as examples, while demonstrating the lack of importance of gender in accounting for overall variability in these traditionally stereotyped areas. (84)

b)   Qualitative research methodologies (e.g., structured interviews) allow a view into experiential data not available through laboratory experimentation. Reinharz (331) and Unger (419) have described qualitative methods, and excellent examples are the work by Keiffer on empowerment (240) and Gilligan on moral reasoning. (157)   The role of experience in the selection of a research topic should be recognized. (160, 430)

c)   The study of change, using a variety of methodologies, is the topic of an issue of the *Journal of Social Issues.* The methods described in this volume include longitudinal analyses and secondary analyses of qualitative and quantitative data. (400)

IV. **New forms of research.** New approaches to science and to research questions are being developed by scholars in the psychology of women. These approaches, often called "feminist science", provide perspective on traditional approaches as well as offering a fresh look at the way we do science within psychology. (238, 268, 313, 331, 338, 419, 430, 447)

V. **Science and the public.** How does society use research results for political ends, especially against women and minorities? (153, 173) How can psychological research, including research on women, affect public policy? (363, 404)

EXERCISES AND ACTIVITIES

1. Critique a study for gender bias, using the guidelines provided earlier. This exercise teaches experimental design as well as general critiquing skills.

2. Using *Psychological Abstracts*, have each student search a specific topic concerning women, such as anorexia. Each student should locate one article on that topic in a journal, and bring it to class. Students can present a brief (1 minute) summary of the theoretical approach, the research approach, and the findings This exercise allows students to use reference resources, and develop search and "brief summary" skills. Class comparisons of different approaches to (and conclusions about) the same topic are instructive.

3. Most experimental psychology classes require research exercises and/or field observations.

   Field research ideas include:
   -- Analysis of portrayals of women in ads by type of product (e.g., computers, medications)
   -- Observations of male/female children's behavior in public places, like fast food restaurants
   -- Content analysis of pictures of women in psychology textbooks
   -- Observations of reactions to male/female infants in a maternity nursery

   Research ideas are plentiful from the psychology of women literature. A standard text in introductory, developmental, or social psychology often offers good ideas. Remember to keep projects simple, with a goal of teaching research skills, not producing a publication.

   -- Replicate the study by Goldberg, "Are women prejudiced against women?", developed into a 1- or 2- independent variable study (sex of subject x sex of hypothetical author). (159)

49

-- Compare "helping behavior" of men and women to a man or woman who is perceived as needing assistance (e.g., who drops a stack of books). References found in chapter on helping behavior in most major social psychology texts. (229)

-- Measure attitudes toward a hypothetical rape victim according to her status, sex of subject, etc. (Original reference (227); use *Social Science Citation Index* for the extensive research modeled on that study).

3. Propose an old saying as a general theory, such as "Success breeds success" or "A clean home is a happy home." Have students explore various ways of testing the theory, including alternative (feminist) research approaches.

4. Hoffnung has discussed various ways to create a classroom atmosphere that promotes gender balance and integration of the psychology of women into experimental psychology, including the world view offered to students. (207)

5. Since Experimental Psychology is a "gateway" course, the class is likely to contain women students making career choices with respect to psychology. Any discussion of career or graduate school plans should consider issues especially important for female students, such as ways to overcome barriers of discrimination. (161, 336, 343, 451)

History of Psychology

TOPICS FOR DISCUSSION

I. **Women of historical importance to psychology.** Identify eminent women in psychology (e.g., the women presidents of American Psychological Association; the women who have won awards from the American Psychological Association and other recognition for distinguished scientific contributions. (37, 45, 56, 94, 147, 148, 306, 359, 368, 375, 381, 399) The history of women (101, 258), of women in the professions (74, 432), and of women in science. (345, 349, 431) Also include the contributions of women in and to psychology.

II. **Contributions of women to psychology.** What are the contributions of women psychologists to the general psychological literature? (147, 182, 368, 399) How have women influenced practices and knowledge in areas such as child development (373), gerontology (Lillian Martin in 53), and mental illness? (89) In what ways have the contributions of women psychologists been lost or ignored or devalued? (45, 92, 110, 120, 359, 364)

III. **Experience of women as psychologists.** Discuss the problems women have overcome in their efforts to become professional psychologists. How did the earlier system of training work for or against women psychologists? How did women succeed in that system? (56, 101, 306, 375, 381, 399, 440) What role have women's organizations (431, 432), women's colleges (387), and Calkins in (399) played in the history of psychology? How have social roles ascribed to women (marriage, motherhood) worked for or against their careers in psychology? (57, 110, 182, 364, 399)

IV. **The study of gender issues in psychology.** Review the psychological study of gender roles and sex differences over the past eight decades, beginning with Wooley (446) and using original source work. (271, 408, 434) Relate the

51

research conclusions to the social and cultural attitudes of
the times (257, 264, 301, 352, 380), and to historical events
like World War II. (364) How has the field of women's
studies changed psychology? (312, 433) Trace the evolution
of a particular gender-related issue, such as the moral
development of men and women, the intellectual abilities of
men and women, childrearing and the attribution of blame to
mothers of abnormal children. (83, 89, 121, 157, 264, 292,
375, 401)

V. **Psychology in historical context.** Philosophical views on
women and on women's education provide a context for
understanding views on women by psychologists. (4, 282,
387) Historical examination of the "sociology of knowledge"
helps develop an "externalist" orientation to the history of
psychology and its treatment of women. (147) The history
of the psychology experiment shows how American
psychologists shifted the emphasis from a study of
intra-individual processes to quantitative intergroup
differences. (105)

EXERCISES AND ACTIVITIES

1. Develop a "Did You Know?" quiz like Russo and O'Connell's about women psychologists and their contributions. Have students give the quiz to faculty or to other advanced psychology students. (Obtain informed consent!) Discuss the results. (364)

2. Interview a woman psychologist trained in the United States prior to 1960, paying special attention to the personal and professional issues she faced, and the career path she elected/was forced to take.

3. Write a biography of a woman psychologist. This could be a class project, with each member bringing an interesting fact about a group-selected individual. This is a good project for teaching archival skills. (356, 409) Benjamin (37) offers an extensive resource list of biographical and autobiographical materials; also see *Notable American Women*, Volumes 1-4.

4. Construct the "typical woman" through her images in the work of early psychologists: for example, masochism (292) or "ideal family". (264) How did psychologists' images compare to social images, obtained through the "women's magazines" of the time (e.g., *Ladies' Home Journal*). Compare the early psychologists' images to contemporary psychologists' views of women, identifying where possible the implications of those early images that are still with us, such as Freud's link of hysteria to "imagined" sexual abuse. (284)

5. Look at several issues of the *Biographical Directory of the American Psychological Association Membership*. Are women's names listed in the early directories? Does the ratio of women to men appear to be stable or changing? For one of the early directories, identify men and women named as Fellows, and see if they are cited in later

historical works. Student should observe a substantial number of women doctorates and contributors (432), but only a small proportion of historical work before 1975 dealing with women. (120, 364)

6.   Hold a mock American Psychological Association Convention from an earlier period, focusing on an issue of special interest such as gender or race differences, using description by Cole. (92) Students can play the role of the psychologist and read a paper based on an original research paper.

7.   Trace the work of a prominent early woman psychologist from first publication through descriptions in texts and citations in reviews.

MEDIA

1. *The Life and Times of Rosie the Riveter.* (1981). Film. World War II roles of women, focusing on their entry into jobs to support the war effort, and their forced exit from the labor market after the war ended. 60 min., Clarity Educational Productions, P.O. Box 315, Franklin Lakes, NJ 07417.

2. *Margaret Mead.* (1960). Film. Documentation of Mead's life and contributions to Psychology and Anthropology, broadcast on Public Broadcasting System. Companion article and transcript available. 30 min., $3, Odyssey, P.O. Box 1000, Boston, MA 02118.

3. *A Visual History of Psychology.* Slides. 140 slides of eminent psychologists and their experiments. Archives of the History of American Psychology, University of Akron, Akron, OH 44325.

Human Sexuality

TOPICS FOR DISCUSSION

I. **Sex and gender.** Differentiate between sex, which refers to sexual anatomy and behavior, and gender, which refers to the state of being male or female. (212, 293) Consider differences in what comprises acceptable male or female behavior as they are influenced by cultural differences and change. (7, 288, 318)

II. **Theories of female sexuality.** Compare Freud's ideas with those of feminists Elizabeth Janeway and Juliet Mitchell. (401)

III. **Sex differences.** What are the real differences between men and women in physiology, personality, and ability? (217, 314, 442)

IV. **Anatomy and physiology.** The debate about female orgasm continues. Is there a difference between clitoral and vaginal orgasm? Discuss sex differences in the experience of multiple orgasm and the possibility of female ejaculation. (243, 285, 318) Describe a pelvic exam. What should be done and why? (59) Note the homologous and analogous organs of the male and female reproductive systems. What are the implications for sexual pleasure in the fact that both have similar origins? Discuss hermaphroditism and accidental excision of the penis during circumcision. What conclusions can you draw with regard to the relative importance of biology (anatomy) and culture? (212, 293)

V. **Menstruation.** Explore the group's awareness of the various terms used to describe menstruation, their origin, and their implications. Do our attitudes shape the words we use or vice versa? (108) Do men and

women have different attitudes toward menstruation?
(164) Discuss menstrual distress: dysmenorrhea and
premenstrual symptoms. What is the etiology: psyche
or soma? (77, 165, 314) There has been a great deal
of discussion about mood change and the menstrual
cycle. What is the magnitude of the mood change and
what effects, if any, have been found on performance?
(104)

VI.   **Menopause.** Separate myth from reality. What is a
hot flash? What are the effects of menopause on
sexuality? (422, 436) Is menopause an illness?
Discuss the politics of menopause. (104)

VII.   **Pregnancy.** What are the common sexual taboos and
fears about sex during pregnancy? When do
gynecologists agree that sex is a no-no? (285)

VIII.   **Contraception.** Why do people who don't want children
fail to use contraception? (367)

IX.   **Abortion.** Who should make the decision about
abortion - the woman, her partner, her parents, the
law? Is it easier for a single woman to justify an
abortion than a married woman? (109, 212)

X.   **Sexual fantasies.** What kind of sexual fantasies do
women have? How do they differ from men's? Why
do some women have rape fantasies? (188, 201, 202)

XI.   **Masturbation.** As a result of "don't look, don't touch"
taboos, many women are reluctant to masturbate and
don't know how. Discuss the Hite Report. (201)

XII.   **Research and attitudes toward virginity.** In studying
sexual behavior among high school and perhaps college
students might you find sex differences in
questionnaire responses that are biased? Are males
more likely to exaggerate and females to minimize
their sexual needs? (442)

XIII.   **Aging.** Who is better able to adjust to aging,
housewives or career women? Is there a double
standard in attractiveness for men and women in terms
of age? (49, 212) Why are we so intolerant of

sexuality in the aging? Why do we assume older people have no sexual needs? (442)

XIV. **Erotica and pornography.** Do women respond to erotica? (19) What is the difference between erotica and pornography? How does pornography harm women? (115)

XV. **Female homosexuality.** How is sexual preference formed? How are gay and straight women alike and in what ways do they differ? (1, 27, 316)

XVI. **Prostitution.** Why would a woman become a prostitute? Who are the clients? (256)

XVII. **Rape.** Rape has been described as the "ultimate violation of the self." What are the known aftereffects experienced by rape victims? (196, 200) Who is the typical rapist? (73) What can a woman do to protect herself against rape? (129)

XVIII. **Love.** Contrary to popular myth, women are less likely to be the first to fall in love. Why might this be so? (435) What do American couples expect from their relationships? (54, 317)

XIX. **Sex therapy.** Orgasmic dysfunction is the most common female sexual problem. Describe the treatment program advocated by Barbach. Why do you think it would or would not work? (20) In what ways are the sexual problems men experience different from those of women and in what ways are they the same? (241)

XX. **Sexually transmitted diseases.** Herpes genitales has reached epidemic proportions in the United States and because it is a recurrent disorder, with no known cure, it is terrifying many young people. Discuss: Prevention and treatment. How do you live with herpes? (186, 210) What can be done to control Acquired Immune Deficiency Syndrome? Separate fact from fiction. (265)

XXI.   **Motherhood.**   What are the current attitudes toward
         motherhood?   What factors influence the decision to
         remain voluntarily childless?   How does fertility affect
         sex role attitudes?   What are the social implications of
         sex choice technology? (358)

EXERCISES AND ACTIVITIES

1. Give the Sex Knowledge Inventories Form X and Form Y and the Sex Attitude Survey and Profile. Useful as an introduction to the discussion of sensitive subjects. An Instructor's manual is available. Source: Family Life Publications, Inc., 219 Henderson St., P.O. Box 427, Saluda, NC 28773.

2. Have each student indicate whether they are male or female. Then have them list what they believe to be the anxieties of men and women in our culture with regard to the size, shape, smell of our genital organs and their function. Suggest that they put an asterisk next to those issues that still concern them. Give feedback regarding how many males worry about penis size, females about breast size, etc. (adapted from Hyde, 1979)

3. Invite a Lamaze instructor to speak to the class about prepared childbirth. If possible, ask her to show a film on prepared childbirth.

4. Invite a LaLeche mother to come to class to describe the organization, a self-help group for nursing mothers that was formed by women who did not get the information that they needed to breast feed successfully from their physicians. Discuss the advantages of breast feeding.

5. Invite a speaker from Planned Parenthood to present alternative methods of birth control, discussing their effectiveness, advantages, and disadvantages. Be sure to request that information about Natural Family Planning is included.

6. Role play abortion dilemmas. Break the class up into groups of four to six people. Have them practice role playing the following situations and any others that you can think of. After about ten minutes have the different groups demonstrate their role plays to the class.

a) A fourteen year old telling her mother that she is pregnant.

b) A twenty year old college student with her boyfriend. Her period is ten days late.

c) A thirty year old mother with two children, aged one and three, discovers that she is pregnant. Family income is limited. She had been planning to return to work as soon as child care arrangements could be made.

d) A thirty-two year old career woman with no desire to marry discovers that she is pregnant.

e) A forty-five year old lawyer finds herself pregnant following a brief romance while away on a business trip. She is married and has two children, one in high school and one in college.

f) A twenty-five year old woman who has been raped learns that she is pregnant.

7. Have students bring in sexual advice columns from *Playboy* or *Viva*. Have small groups discuss and evaluate the advice given.

8. Have the groups share childhood sexual experiences such as: "The first time I heard about sexual intercourse..."

9. Check out sex role stereotypes by having the class free associate to

Women are _____
Men are _____

10. Record a talk show discussion of sexuality and bring into class for discussion. Consider the value of instant sexual advice.

11. Give the Bem Androgyny Scale. (32, 216)

12. Collect anti-gay humor on TV comedy shows. Compare with anti-women jokes. What are the stereotypes reflected? If you were a gay person listening to these jokes, how would you feel?

13. Role play a college senior telling her parents that she is gay. Would it be easier for a thirty-five year old male physician?

14. Role play a couple with sex problems. He has premature ejaculations. She has difficulty reaching orgasm.

15. Role play or discuss as a group: How to tell your nine year old daughter about sex. Then tell your nine year old son.

MEDIA

1. *A Ripple of Time.* (1974). Film. Lovemaking of a mature couple, ages fifty and sixty-three. Sexually explicit. 24 min., color, $50, Multi Media Resource Center, 1525 Franklin Street, San Francisco, CA 94109.

2. *Becoming Orgasmic: A Sexual Growth Program for Women.* Film. A series of three films. The first demonstrates self discovery, the second self pleasuring, and the third introduces the woman's partner. If only one film can be used, Film III *Sharing* is suggested. 18 min., color, $50, Focus International Inc., 1 East 53rd Street, New York, NY 10022.

3. *Four Young Women.* Film. First person descriptions of the decision to have an abortion. 20 min., color, $28.50, Perennial Education, Inc., 477 Roger Williams, P.O. Box 855, Ravinia, Highland Park, IL 60035.

4. *Hookers.* (1975). Film. A controversial documentary about prostitution. 25 min., color, $55, Multi Media Resource Center, 1525 Franklin Street, San Francisco, CA 94109.

5. *I Change I Am the Same.* Film. A woman and a man in their own and each other's clothing. Very funny. 40 seconds, b/w, $12, Multi Media Resource Center, 1525 Franklin Street, San Francisco, CA 94109.

6. *Jennifer.* (1982). Film. A young woman trying to cope with her own case of genital herpes. 28 min., color, free. Modern Talking Pictures Scheduling Department, 5000 Park Street North, St. Petersburg, FL 33709.

7. *Lavender.* (1972). Film. Describes the lives of two young lesbians. 13 min., color, $17, Perennial Education, Inc., 477 Roger Williams, P.O. Box 855, Ravinia, Highland Park, IL 60035.

8. *Like Other People.* Sexual needs of the physically handicapped are conveyed by a couple with cerebral palsy. 37 min., color, $37.50, Perennial Education, Inc., 477 Roger Williams, P.O. Box 855, Ravinia, Highland Park, IL 60035.

9. *Near the Big Chakra.* (1972). Film. Presentation of the vulvas of thirty-eight women ranging in age from six months to fifty-six years. 15 min., color, $40, Multi Media Resource Center, 1525 Franklin Street, San Francisco, CA 94109.

10. *Straight Talk About Lesbians.* Filmstrip with cassette. A sound filmstrip that dispels myths and explores lesbian lifestyles. Women's Educational Media Inc., 47 Cherry Street, Somerville, MA 02144.

11. *Susan.* (1971). Film. Female masturbation using vibrator, running water, and manual stimulation. Sexually explicit. 16 min., color, $40, Multi Media Resource Center, 1525 Franklin Street, San Francisco, CA 94109.

12. *Talking about Breastfeeding.* Film. A number of women describe their experiences and ways in which they dealt with common problems. 17 min., color, $30, Polymorph Films, 118 South Street, Boston, MA 02111.

13. *Women: The Hand That Cradles the Rock.* Film. Presents different view of women's roles, marriage, and childrearing. 20 min., color, Document Associates, Inc., 800 Third Ave., New York, NY 10022.

14. *Love in Later Life.* (1983). Film. A couple now in their seventies describe their life together. They are seen talking, touching, making love. Counters taboos about older people's sexuality. 30 min., color, $65, Multi Media Resource Center, 1525 Franklin Street, San Francisco, CA 94109.

Learning and Motivation

I. **Definition.** "Learning refers to the change in a Subject's behavior or behavior potential to a given situation brought about by the Subject's repeated experiences in that situation, provided that the behavior change cannot be explained on the basis of the Subject's native response tendencies, maturation, or temporary states (such as fatigue, drunkenness, drives and so on)." Is this definition adequate? (62, p. 11)

II. **Laws of learning.** Most learning theory texts (e.g., 62) distinguish between the effects of learning and the effects of maturation, habituation, species-specific behavior and temporary states such as fatigue or druggedness. Do these other factors interact with learning; if so, are the laws of learning general? Seligman (372) argues, for example, that the laws of learning may change according to the biological preparedness of an organism to effect a response to a stimulus. (55, 64) Training tactics may change for prepared, contraprepared, or neutral responses.

III. **Biology and ability.** Is Seligman's argument another way of saying anatomy is destiny or a way of respectfully acknowledging individual differences including sex differences? (272)

IV. **Learning and performance.** Most learning texts also introduce a distinction between learning (what is acquired) and performance (what is demonstrated). Variables intervening between learning and performance include motivation to perform, expectation of reward of performing, and current ability to perform because of personal qualities and the nature of the task. Discuss the implications for knowledge vs. performance of behaviors inconsistent with sex role. Analyze examples from the literature on achievement motivation in men and women. (98, 209, 220)

Analyze expressed aggression in men and women. (102, 122) Analyze attribution of causation for success and failure in men and women. (151, 302)

V. **Connectionist and cognitive approaches.** Is behaviorism "a political science of contingent influence?" Who controls the major secondary reinforcers, social approval and money, in our current culture? (183) Perceived control of events, and mastery have been related to self esteem. (137) Learned helplessness has been related to feelings of depression. (62) What socialization styles are associated with feelings of mastery or helplessness? (137) Cognitive theories assume that sensory representations of environmental influences are processed and arranged by an active intellect. Is there evidence for differences in the organization and processing capabilities of men and women? (76, 78, 131, 162, 169, 177, 214, 272, 300, 394, 444) If such differences exist, what are the implications for individualized approaches to education? (131, 151, 272, 300, 444)

VI. **Motivation.** What are optimal levels of arousal, direction, and persistance in behavior? Are there sex differences in curiosity, creativity, or search for novelty? (194, 273) Consider the nature of the psychological and biological regulation of sexual behavior. (137) What makes a person socially or sexually desirable? Discuss the characteristics of men and women as models and goal objects. (62, 332)

EXERCISES AND ACTIVITIES

1. Recall the last time you performed poorly. What is your reason for it? Are there sex differences in the class? Are these differences consistent with gender and attribution?

2. Keep a log for a day. Who rewards whom? For what? How? Do females give and seek more social rewards while men emphasize tangible rewards? To what extent is your own behavior controlled by contingencies you now perceive?

3. Are there gender differences in the conditions under which males and females work most effectively? How does this relate to the literature on fear of success and fear of failure?

4. Estimate your score on the next exam. Record the discrepancy. Are there sex differences in estimations in the classroom?

MEDIA

1. *Creative Problem Solving.* (1980). Film. Discusses creativity and split-brain research, the origin of ideas, brainstorming techniques, synectics, and the relationship of creativity to self confidence. 28 min., Color, CRM, Rental $33, Film Rental Center, Syracuse University, 1455 East Colvin Street, Syracuse, NY 13210.

2. *Development of the Child: A Cross-Cultural Approach to Cognition.* (1975). Film. Rate of development of age-related skills in three widely different cultures. 20 min., color, Rental $13, University of Illinois Film Center, 1325 South Oak Street, Champaign, IL 61820.

3. *Development of the Child: A Cross-Cultural Approach to the Acquisition of Sex Roles and Social Standards.* (1975). Film. A comparison of sex-typing, use of verbal and physical punishment in three cultures: rural Kenya, urban Japanese, and Guatemalan Indian. 23 min., color, Rental $15, University of Illinois Film Center, 1325 South Oak Street, Champaign, IL 61820.

4. *Learning.* (1971). Film. This is a sexist film. It presents a slick review of supra-normal releasing stimuli (a female bosom on Wall Street), conditioned fear (acquired to rabbits, lust to Playboy Bunnies). It is listed here as a vehicle to examine media for sexist presentation of scholarly material. After a discussion on sexism, the class can proceed to discuss Skinner and McClelland's presentations, aggression in rats, imprinting and the other phenomena presented in this fast-paced film. 30 minutes, color, Rental $16.50, University of Illinois Film Center, 1325 South Oak Street, Champaign, IL 61820.

5. *Productivity and the Self-Fulfilling Prophecy: The Pygmalion Effect.* (1974). Film. Rosenthal discusses the power of expectations. 30 min., color, Rental $17.50, University of Illinois Film Center, 1325 South Oak Street, Champaign, IL 61820.

6. *Token Economics: Behaviorism Applied.* (1973). Film. Skinner introduces this film. Prisoners, retardates, old people, orphaned children, and psychotics are the subject groups of the helpless. 23 min., color, Rental $20, Film Rental Center, Syracuse University, 1455 East Colvin Street, Syracuse, NY 13210.

Social Psychology

TOPICS FOR DISCUSSION

I. **Sexism in psychological research.** How do stereotypic ideas influence the questions that are investigated scientifically? Does bias exist in the choice of subjects used for psychological research? Is there bias in the interpretation of research findings? (145, 328)

II. **Impression management and attribution.** What is beauty? How do we decide who is beautiful? And how does physical attractiveness influence our lives? (46) Women are more likely to attribute their success to luck, whereas men attribute success to their own abilities. Why might this be so and what effect could it have on females' own expectations of success? (106, 216) What is the effect of using cosmetics on getting dates or jobs? (97, 142)

III. **Communication.** Men and women's nonverbal and verbal patterns of behavior differ. In what ways do these differences affect social interaction? Who asks more questions? Are males or females more likely to interrupt the opposite sex? (106, 145, 195, 250)

IV. **Interpersonal relations, liking, and loving.** It is interesting to focus on the norms surrounding dating behavior. What should a woman who is interested in dating a particular man do? Ask him out? Hint? Nothing? Is it true that men are more romantic than women? Are women more likely to have stronger loving feelings toward same-sex friends? (106, 256, 355)

V. **Sex and sex roles.** Differentiate between sex and gender. Discuss the statement: "Men: They're all the same." or "Women: They're all the same." (34, 35, 106, 355) How do the sexes differ in response to sexual stimulation? In the use of fantasy? (216) Women may be seen as both sexual criminals and victims. This is not usually true for men. Discuss why this is so. (Prostitution and rape are issues here.) (107, 115, 256)

VI.   **Aggression.** Are women always less aggressive than men? What are the consequences of aggressive behavior for women and for men? (106, 145, 146, 355) There is a relationship between intimacy and aggression in which women fare poorly. Discuss the life situation of battered wives. (280)

VII.   **Prosocial behavior.** Women are more commonly seen as nurturant. What are the implications of this stereotype for the nurturant man or the non-nurturant woman? (34) Burnout is a phenomenon that affects those in the helping professions, though it has recently been generalized to include other areas. Are men or women more susceptible to burnout and why? (106, 283)

VIII.   **Prejudice.** Differentiate between prejudice, discrimination, racism, and sexism. Discuss some common stereotypes of women, blacks, hispanics, and others as portrayed in the media. (106, 145, 407) Describe some of the similarities between blacks and women as they relate to both groups as the objects of discrimination. For example, visible characteristics, psychological characteristics, behaviors used to cope with discrimination. (216) Are minority women subject to the double whammy: prejudice as women and as members of a minority group? (2, 23, 34, 82, 96, 295, 413)

IX.   **Attitudes.** In what ways do attitudes adversely affect women's occupational aspirations and work behavior? (307)

X.   **Conformity.** Women are more easily influenced than men. True or false? (119)

XI.   **Leadership and group behavior.** The predominance of males in leadership positions is a reflection of the natural order of things. Defend or refute. (106, 167, 232)

XII.   Morality.   Freud said that women's super-ego development was never as complete as that of men. Thus women are morally less well developed. What have researchers such as Kohlberg found and what does Gilligan present in her alternative view? (135, 137)

EXERCISES AND ACTIVITIES

1. Assign an experiment using non-obtrusive measures in which students observe sex differences. For example: Sex differences in smoking behavior in the cafeteria; sex differences in greeting behavior (who touches whom and where); sex differences in touching a stuffed animal placed on a cafeteria table.

2. Explore physical attractiveness using the experiment described by Wrightsman in the *Study Guide for Social Psychology* (Brooks/Cole), pages 33-42, "The Case of Helen Forbes."

3. Role play assertive vs. aggressive responses to various common situations: Confronting a teacher or an employer. Refusing a request. Asking a favor.

   Role play:
   a)   a sexist job interview
   b)   an episode of sexual harassment

4. Design a campaign, using information about attitude change, to promote the Equal Rights Amendment, or to initiate an equal opportunity program in a business organization you know.

5. Create a non-sexist TV commercial for an imaginary product.

6. Do the Bem Sex Role Inventory or a Sex Reversal Guided Fantasy.

7. Ba Fa Ba Fa. A cross-culture simulation. Participants live and cope in an artificially contrived culture. There are two cultures in the simulation. In one of them females are obviously, of little importance. Can be done in a fifty minute period and discussed during the next class. A two hour period is better. Available from Simile 11, P.O. Box

910, Del Mar, CA   92014.   Purchase price is $35.   Materials may be reused.

8.   The Academic Game.   Designed by Bredemaier, O'Connell, Unger, et al.   A simulation demonstrating the methods and result of sexism in academia.   Available from Institute of Higher Education Research and Services, P.O. Box 6293, University, AL   35486.

MEDIA

1. *Ain't Nobody's Business But My Own.* Film. Documentary about female prostitution. Shatters some stereotypic views of prostitutes. 54 min., color, Mountain Moving Pictures Company, 1910 Weepah Way, Hollywood, CA 90046.

2. *Cat:A Woman Who Fought Back.* (1978). Film. Story of a twenty-four year old woman boxer who fights to strike down laws preventing women from boxing professionally. Entertaining. 27 min., color, Women Make Movies, Inc., 257 West 19th Street, New York, NY 10011.

3. *Chicana.* Film. A documentary that surveys Chicana history from pre-Columbian time to the present. 22 min., Sylvia Morales, c/o KCET, 4401 Sunset Bl., Los Angeles, CA 90027.

4. *Communication: The Nonverbal Agenda.* (1974). Film. Examples of non-verbal messages conveyed during interviews and male-female encounters in social situations. 30 min., color, Contemporary/McGraw-Hill Films, 1221 Avenue of the Americas, New York, NY 10020.

5. *Female Genesis.* (1973). Slides. Cartoon presentation of the creation of women and the strings attached to her enjoyment of sexuality. Humorous view of sexual taboos. 24 slides, color. Multi Media Resource Center, 1525 Franklin Street, San Francisco, CA 94109.

6. *Issues in Sexual Behavior.* Three film strips with Cassettes. Topics include: Rape, Prostitution, and Homosexuality. May be used separately or together. Each explores facts, attitudes, and theories pertaining to each subject and presents alternative points of view. Good presentation of the issue of personal freedom vs. social pressure. College Division, Harper and Row Media, 10 East 53rd Street, New York, NY 10022.

7. *Killing Us Softly: Advertising's Image of Women.*   Film.
    Using ads, Jean Kilborne shows how powerfully they
    condition our beliefs about women.   30 min., color,
    Cambridge, Documentary Films, Inc., P.O. Box 385,
    Cambridge, MA 02139.

8. *Men's Lives.* (1974). Film. Shows how American boys are
    programmed to become men: not to show emotion, be
    aggressive and competitive. New Day Films, P.O. Box 315,
    Franklin Lakes, NJ 07417.

9. *Rape Culture.* Film. Portrayal of media treatment of rape
    and the experiences of rapists, victims, and rape crisis
    workers. 35 min., Cambridge Documentary Films, Inc., P.O.
    Box 385, Cambridge, MA 02139.

10. *Sex Role Development.* (1974). Film. Transmission to
    children of sex role stereotypes. Presents alternatives. 23
    min., color, Contemporary/McGraw-Hill Films, 1221 Avenue
    of the Americas, New York, NY 10020.

11. *The Gentle Art of Saying No.* Three Filmstrips with
    Cassettes or LP Records. Differentiates between assertive,
    non-assertive, and aggressive behaviors.   Demonstrates
    assertive behavior in a variety of situations. 40 min., color,
    Sunburst Communications, Dept. STG, 41 Washington Ave.,
    Pleasantville, NY 10570.

12. *This Ad Insults Women.* Filmstrip. (Part of The Silenced
    Majority, a five part filmstrip-cassette package).
    Demonstrates sexism in advertising. Media Plus Inc., 60
    Riverside Drive, New York, NY 10024.

13. *Women in Management: Threat or Opportunity.* (1974).
    Film. The effect of the women's movement on business.
    Changing perceptions of women's roles. In-service training
    program. 27 min., color, Contemporary/McGraw-Hill Films,
    1221 Avenue of the Americas, New York, NY 10020.

14. *Yes Baby, She's My Sir.* Filmstrip with Cassette.
    Demonstrates sexist language and the way in which language
    affects women's goals, behavior, and self-concepts. Feminist
    Productions, Inc., 31 Greenway South, Babylon, NY 11702.

15. *Silent Pioneers.* (1985) Film or Videocassette. A diverse
    group of gay and lesbian older people challenge stereotypes

about homosexuals. 42 min., color, Filmakers Library, Inc., 133 East 58th Street, New York, NY 10022.

16. *We're Here Now.* (1981). Film or Videocassette. Seven former prostitutes describe their exploitation by pimps and customers and struggles to return to the mainstream of society. Shows prostitutes as real people. 35 min., color, Filmakers Library, Inc., 133 East 58th Street, New York, NY 10022.

Statistics

I. **Feelings about taking Statistics.** Are there sex-related differences in admitted anxiety in this class? (203) Statistics is a tool of mathematically precise argument. What have researchers, using statistics, told us about sex differences in math and problem-solving? (71, 219, 271, 449) If there are demonstrated sex differences in math and problem-solving, regardless of their origin, what can one do about it? (15, 75, 203, 325, 449)

II. **Scales of measurement.** The use of nominal, ordinal, interval, or ratio scales often implies a theory about the nature of what is being measured. In research, we strive for isomorphism between what we measure and how we measure it. For example, can sex (M, F) be conceived of *only* as a nominal variable? (32, 144, 176, 293)

III. **Independent and dependent variables.** Predictors and criteria. The definition and choice of variables often reflect the assumptions, values, even biases of experimenters. When is it appropriate and when is it inappropriate to study sex differences? (270, 405) Do "sex differences" reflect only differences in sex? (144, 176, 270, 271, 410) Is "sex" a precisely defined variable? (145, 176, 293)

IV. **Sampling.** When are samples representative? When are single sex samples appropriate or inappropriate? (270, 271, 405) Experimenters sample not only subjects, but content, constructs, and measures. Psychological research is characterized by two sampling styles -- many measures of a few people (fidelity) vs. few measures of many people (bandwidth). With limited resources one must opt for bandwidth or fidelity but not both. (99, 100) The style of research in fields with many women -- developmental, clinical -- tends to emphasize fidelity. (373) Discuss the implications.

V. **Type I and Type II error.** In adopting a p level, the social consequences of making Type I or Type II error must be addressed. What are the consequences of assuming sex differences in math ability are genetic when they may not be vs. assuming they are not genetic when they may be? (29, 214, 289)

VI. **Interpreting results.** To control for biases of interpretation, the student may practice formulating plausible rival hypotheses to account for the data. These hypotheses may include the effects of the statistic used, the effects of operational definitions of variables, the effects of procedures used to carry out the study, and the effects of adopting alternative value stances to interpret results. (81, 145, 289, 410) Present and follow an argument over the interpretation of results. Broverman et al. (71) vs. Parlee (311) is a useful discussion of sex differences in cognitive abilities. For examples of well thought out research, consult Tanur et al. (405)

EXERCISES AND ACTIVITIES

1. Compute the grade point averages for quantitative and for other courses for students in the class. Compare (tdep). Compute each student's GPA from male and female professors. Compare (2 x 2 ANOVA with repeated measures on professors, factorial for sex of subject).

2. Analyze the men's and women's winning times for the New York Marathon over the last ten years. Discuss choice of statistics for sexist (tdep) and egalitarian (r) arguments from the data. Discuss alternate interpretations of data, with some reflecting biological differences (length of shin bone, distribution of body fat) while others reflect social forces (training time). Suggest future research to investigate alternate hypotheses.

3. Predict the women's winning time for ten years hence. Discuss errors of measurement, linearity, asymptotes, intervening variables. Compare to men's past times. Use common sense to select the data used for prediction and to evaluate the answer.

4. Use statistical techniques to show if there has been significant change in the last forty years in opinions about voting for a qualified woman for president. (405)

5. Have students predict their performance in this course at the beginning of the semester. Compute test average. Correlate achievement and expectations. Are there gender differences in accuracy of prediction?

REFERENCE SECTION

1. Abbott, S., & Love, B. (1973). *Sappho was a right-on woman.* New York: Stein & Day.

2. Acosta-Belen, E. (1979). *The Puerto Rican woman.* New York: Praeger.

3. Adler, N. (1981). Sex roles and unwanted pregnancy in adolescent and adult women. *Professional Psychology, 12,* 56-66.

4. Agonito, R. (1977). *History of Ideas on women: A source book.* New York: G. P. Putnam.

5. Aldous, J. (Ed.). (1982). *Two paychecks: Life in dual-career families.* Beverly Hills, CA: Sage. Critically examines implications of the interface between family and job roles and issues relating to the interaction of family members when both spouses are earners.

6. Allen, W. R. (1979). Family roles, occupational statuses, and achievement orientations among black women in the United States. *Signs, 4,* 670-686.

7. Allgeier, E. R., & McCormick, N. P. (Eds.). (1983). *Changing boundaries.* Palo Alto, CA: Mayfield.

8. American Psychological Association. (1975). Report of the task force on sex biases and sex-role stereotyping in psychotherapeutic practice. *American Psychologist, 30,* 1169-1175.

9.____. (1978a). Guidelines for therapy with women. *American Psychologist, 33,* 1122.

10. ——. Division 17 Ad Hoc Committee on Women. (1978b).
Principles concerning the counseling and psychotherapy of
women. *Counseling Psychologist*, 8(1), 21.

11. ——. (1981a). Ethical principles of psychologists (revised).
American Psychologist, 36, 633-638.

12. ——. (1981b). *Report of the Division 17 Committee on
Women Task Force on Training for Counseling Women.*
(Available from Mary Sue Richardson, Department of
Counselor Education, New York University, New York, NY
10003.)

13. Andrade, S. J. (1982). Social science stereotypes of the
Mexican-American woman: Policy implications for research.
Hispanic Journal of Behavioral Sciences, 4(2), 223-244.

14. Aneshensel, C., Frerichs, R., & Clark, V. (1981). Family
roles and sex differences in depression. *Journal of Health
and Social Behavior, 22*, 379-393.

15. Arkin, M., & Shollar, B. (1982). *The tutor book.* New York:
Longman, Inc.
Accompanied by a pamphlet specific to math tutoring, *The
math tutor,* this is a guide for training peer tutors. The
mathematics pamphlet covers math anxiety, math avoidance,
common math misconceptions, learning styles, and use of
tacit knowledge. The training guide emphasizes respect and
communication among teacher, tutor, and student. Well-
chosen literary excerpts portray both men and women as
learners or teachers, experiencing and overcoming difficulty.

16. Arms, S. (1975). *Immaculate deception.* New York: Bantam
Books.

17. Auerbach, K. (1984). Employed breastfeeding mothers:
Problems they encounter. *Birth: Issues in Prenatal Care &
Education, 11*, 17-20.

18. Bachrach, L. (1984). Deinstitutionalization and women:
Assessing the consequences of public policy. *American
Psychologist, 39*, 1171-1177.

19. Baker, S. (1985). Biological influences on human sex and gender. In J. H. Williams (Ed.), *Psychology of women: Selected readings (Second Ed.)* (pp. 80-94). New York: Norton.

20. Barbach, L. G. (1975). *For yourself· The fulfillment of female sexuality*. New York: Doubleday.

21. Barnett, R. (1982). Multiple roles and well-being: A study of mothers of preschool age children. *Psychology of Women Quarterly, 7,* 175-178.

22. Barrett, C. (1981). Intimacy in widowhood. *Psychology of Women Quarterly, 5(3),* 473-478.

23. Batille, G. (1980). Bibliography on Native American women. *Concerns*, 10(2).
    Available from Concerns, 405 Elmside Bl., Madison, WI, 53704.

24. Baumrind, D. (1972). From each according to her ability. *School Review*, 80, 161-197.
    Exploration of socialization factors which produce greater instrumental competence in boys.

25. ———. (1982). Are androgynous individuals more effective persons and parents? *Child Development, 53,* 44-75.

26. Bayley, S., Morris, J., & Sheppard, J. (1983). Sexism in schools. *American Educational Research Journal, 6,* 12-17.

27. Bell, A. P., Weinberg, M. S., & Hammersmith, S. K. (1981). *Sexual preference*. Bloomington, IN: Indiana University Press.

28. Bell, I. P. (1979). The double standard: Age. In J. Freeman (Ed.), *Women: A feminist perspective*, 2nd. edition, (pp. 233-242). Palo Alto, CA: Mayfield Pub.

29. Bell, E. T. (1965). *Men of mathematics*. New York: Simon and Schuster.
    Despite the title, this set of biographies of the "greatest" mathematicians contains the story of *one woman*, Sonja Kowalewski, pp. 423-432. A Professor of Mathematics Weierstrass, Sonja was both a novelist and mathematician. She is included in these references in the belief that every

gifted woman needs a role model. Her major mathematics prize was won for a paper submitted anonymously.

30. Belle, D. (Ed.). (1982). *Lives in stress: Women and depression.* Beverly Hills, CA: Sage.

31. ———. (1984). Inequality and mental health: Low income and minority women. In L. E. Walker, (Ed.), *Women and mental health policy.* Beverly Hills: Sage.

32. Bem, S. L. (1974). The measurement of psychological androgyny. *Journal of Consulting and Clinical Psychology, 42,* 155-162. The concept of masculinity-femininity as a continuum is attacked.

33. ———. (1975). Androgyny vs. the tight little lives of fluffy women and chesty men. *Psychology Today, 9*(4), 58.

34. ———. (1976). Probing the promise of androgyny. In A. G. Kaplan & J. P. Bean (Eds.), *Beyond sex-role stereotypes* (pp. 47-62). Boston: Little Brown.
    An introduction to the concept of psychological androgyny. Summary of research using the Bem Sex-Role Inventory.

35. ———. (1983). Gender schema theory and its implications for child development: Raising gender-aschematic children in a gender-schematic society. *Signs: Journal of Women in Culture and Society, 8*(4), 598-616.

36. Benbow, C. P., & Stanley, J. C. (1983). Sex differences in mathematical reasoning ability: More facts. *Science, 222,* 1029-1030.

37. Benjamin, L. T. (1980). Women in psychology: Biography and autobiography. *Psychology of Women Quarterly, 5,* 140-144.

38. Bennett, B., & Reardon, R. (1985). Dual-career couples and the psychological adjustment of offspring: A review. *School Counselor, 32,* 287-295.

39. Benz, C. R., Pfeiffer, I., & Newman, I. (1981). Sex role expectations of classroom teachers, grades 1-12. *American Educational Research Journal, 18,* 289-302.

40. Bernard, J. (1975a). *The future of motherhood.* New York: Penguin.

41. ———. (1975b). *Women, wives and mother.* Chicago: Aldine Pub.

42. ———. (1979). The mother role. In J. Freeman (Ed.), *Women: A feminist perspective* (pp. 122-133). Palo Alto, CA: Mayfield.

43. Bernardez, T. (1983). Women's groups. In M. Rosenbaum (Ed.), *Handbook of short-term therapy groups* (pp. 119-138). New York: McGraw-Hill.

44. ———. (1984). Prevalent disorders of women: Attempts toward a different understanding and treatment. *Women and Therapy, 3*(3/4), 17-28.

45. Bernstein, M. D., & Russo, N. F. (1974). The history of psychology revisited: Or, up with our foremothers. *American Psychologist, 29,* 130-134.

46. Berscheid, E., & Walster, E. (1982). Beauty and the best. In D. Krebs (Ed.), *Readings in social psychology* (pp. 192-196). New York: Harper & Row.
The impact of physical attractiveness from early childhood through adulthood.

47. Best, R. (1983). *We've all got scars: What boys and girls learn in elementary school.* Bloomington, IN: Indiana University Press.

48. Billingsley, D. (1977). Sex bias in psychotherapy: An examination of the effects of client sex, client pathology, and therapist sex on treatment planning. *Journal of Consulting and Clinical Psychology, 45*(12), 250-256.

49. Birnbaum, J. (1976). Life patterns and self esteem in gifted family-oriented and career-oriented women. In M. Mednich, L. W. Hoffman, & S. Tangri (Eds.), *Woman: Social psychological perspectives on achievement.* New York: Psychological Dimensions.

50. Bledsoe, J. C. (1983). Sex differences in female teachers' approval and disapproval behaviors as related to their definition of sex-role type. *Psychological Reports, 53,* (3, Pt. 1), 711-714.

51. Block, J. H. (1973). Conception of sex roles: Some cross cultural and longitudinal perspectives. *American Psychologist, 28,* 512-526.

52. ———. (1976). Issues, problems, and pitfalls in assessing sex differences: A critical review of "The Psychology of Sex Differences." *Merrill-Palmer Quarterly, 22,* 283-308.

53. Block, M. (Ed.). (1942). *Current biography.* New York: The H. W. Wilson Company.

54. Blumstein, P., & Schwartz, P. (1983). *American couples.* New York: William Morrow.

55. Bolles, R. (1970). Species-specific defense reaction in avoidance learning. *Psychological Review, 71,* 32-48. Species specific defense reactions are "prepared" for learning in avoidance learning paradigms.

56. Boring, E. G. (1951). The woman problem. *American Psychologist, 6,* 679-682.

57. ———. (1952). *A history of psychology in autobiography,* Vol. 4. Worcester, MA: Clark University Press.

58. Boskind-Lodahl, M. (1976). Cinderella's stepsister: A feminist perspective on anorexia nervosa and bulimia. *Signs, 2,* 120-146.
The attempt of young women to fit themselves into an emaciated mold.

59. Boston Women's Health Book Collective. (1984). *The new our bodies, ourselves.* New York: Simon & Schuster.

60. Bouhoutsos, J. C. (1984). Sexual intimacy between psychotherapists and clients: Policy implications for the future. In L. E. Walker (Ed.), *Women and mental health policy.* Beverly Hills: Sage.

61. Bouhoutsos, J., Holroyd, J., Lerman, H., Forer, B., & Greenberg, M. (1983). Sexual intimacy between psychotherapists and patients. *Professional Psychology: Research and Practice, 14*(2), 185-196.

62. Bower, G., & Hilgard, E. (1981). *Theories of learning.* Fifth Edition. Englewood Cliffs, NJ: Prentice-Hall.
The latest edition of the classic learning text, it has no section on sex differences, except differences in sexual behavior.

63. Brannon, R. (1981). Current methodological issues in paper-and- pencil measuring instruments. *Psychology of Women Quarterly, 5,* 618-627.

64. Breland, K., & Breland, M. (1960). The misbehavior of organisms. *American Psychologist, 16,* 661-664.
The Brelands illustrate how innate responses constrain and interfere with operantly conditioned responses.

65. Brodsky, A. (1973). The consciousness-raising group as a model of therapy with women. *Psychotherapy: Theory, Research and Practice, 10*(1), 24-29.

66. ———. (1977). Countertransference issues and the woman therapist: Sex and the student therapist. *The Clinical Psychologist, 30*(2), 12-14.

67. ———. (1980). A decade of feminist influence on psychotherapy. *Psychology of Women Quarterly, 4*(3), 331-344.

68. ———. (1982). Sex, race, and class in psychotherapy research. In J. Harvey & M. Parks (Eds.), *Psychotherapy research and behavior change: Master Lecture Series, Vol. 1,* (pp. 123-150). Washington, D.C.: American Psychological Association.

69. Brodsky, A., & Hare-Mustin, R. (Eds.). (1980). *Women and psychotherapy: An assessment of research and practice.* New York: Guilford.
Five topic areas are discussed: research in gender differences in therapy, traditional psychotherapeutic approaches, high-prevalence disorders, evaluation of crisis intervention for women, and alternative psychotherapeutic approaches.

70. Brody, C. M. (Ed.). (1984). *Women therapists working with women: New theory and process of feminist theory.* New York: Springer.

71. Broverman, D., Klaiber, E., Kobayashi, Y., & Vogel, W.
    (1968). Roles of activation and inhibition in sex differences
    in cognitive abilities. *Psychological Review, 75*(1), 23-50.
    An argument for biologically based differences in men's and
    women's cognitive abilities is put forth. It is scientific and
    convincing until the student reads Parlee's reply.

72. Brown, L. S. (1984). Finding a new language: Getting beyond
    analytic verbal shorthand in feminist therapy. *Women and
    Therapy, 3*, 73-80.

73. Brownmiller, S. (1975). *Against our will: Men, women, and
    rape.* New York: Simon & Schuster.

74. Brumberg, J. J., & Tomes, N. (1982). Women in the
    professions: A research agenda for American historians.
    Reviews in American History, 7, 275-296.

75. Bruning, J., & Kintz, B. (1977). *Computational handbook of
    statistics.* Glenview, IL: Scott Foresman & Co.
    A practical book designed to reduce math anxiety, useful as
    an accompaniment to a text. Each section introduces a
    statistic, its assumptions, uses and limitations. An example
    is worked out step by step. The book proceeds from
    organizing and graphing data to a thorough treatment of
    Analysis of Variance. Classroom-tested at a women's
    college.

76. Bryden, M. P. (1979). Evidence of sex-related differences in
    cerebral organization. In M. Wittig & A. Petersen (Eds.),
    Sex related differences in cognitive functioning (pp. 121-
    144). San Francisco: Academic Press.
    Presents evidence that men may have greater cerebral
    hemisphere lateralization than women leading to superior
    performance on some tasks. Documents sex-related
    differences in cerebral anatomy and response to cerebral
    damage.

77. Budoff, P. (1981). *No more menstrual cramps.* New York:
    Penguin.

78. Burstein, B., Bank, L., & Jarvik, L. (1980). Sex differences
    in cognitive functioning: Evidence, determinants,
    implications. *Human Development, 23*, 289-313.
    Reviews the literature on hormonal aberrations and test
    performance, cognitive style and sex differences. The
    authors conclude there is evidence of sex differences in

cognitive functioning, but little evidence to indicate the etiology of those differences.

79. Burtle, V. (1978). *Women who drink: Alcoholic experience and psychotherapy.* Springfield, IL: Charles C. Thomas. Considers the major issues in studying women alcoholics. It includes a literature review, case studies, a discussion of minority women, and a study of how socialization patterns may contribute to later alcoholism.

80. Cammaert, L. P. (1984). New sex therapies: Policy and practice. In L. E. Walker (Ed.), *Women and mental health policy* (pp. 247-266). Beverly Hills, CA: Sage.

81. Campbell, D., & Stanley, J. (1966). *Experimental and quasi-experimental designs for research.* Chicago: R. McNally. Advocates value-fair (as opposed to value free) design and interpretation of experiments through the use of competing plausible hypotheses. Points out common sources which cloud interpretation of experimental results such as subject selection biases, maturation of subjects, etc.

82. Candelaria, C. (Ed.). (1980, Summer). Chicanas in the national landscape. Special issue of *Frontiers: A Journal of Women's Studies, 5*(2).

83. Caplan, P. J., & Hall-McCorquodale, I. H. (1985). Mother-blaming in major clinical journals. *American Journal of Orthopsychiatry, 55*(3), 345-353.

84. Caplan, P. J., MacPherson, G. M., & Tobin, P. (1985). Do sex-related differences in spatial abilities exist? A multilevel critique with new data. *American Psychologist, 40,* 786-799.

85. Carlson, R. (1972). Understanding women: Implications for personality theory and research. *Journal of Social Issues, 28*(2), 17-33.

86. Carmen, E. H., & Reiker, P. P. (Eds.). (1984). *The gender gap in psychotherapy: Social realities and psychological processes.* New York: Plenum. Designed for teaching courses on mental health and women, this volume contains an excellent compilation of some of the best of the writing in the area, many of them listed separately in this bibliography.

87. Carmen, E., Russo, N., & Miller, J. (1981). Inequality and women's mental health: An overview. *American Journal of Psychiatry, 138,* 1319-1330.

88. Chafetz, J. (1978). *Masculine/feminine or human?* Itasca, IL: Peacock.

89. Chesler, P. (1972). *Women and madness.* New York: Doubleday.

90. Chess, S., & Thomas, A. (1984). Infant bonding: Mystique and reality. *Annual Progress in Child Psychiatry & Child Development,* 48-62.

91. Chico, N. P., & Hartley, S. F. (1981). Widening choices in motherhood of the future. *Psychology of Women Quarterly, 6,* 12-25.

92. Cole, D. L. (1983). The way we were: Teaching history of psychology through mock APA conventions. *Teaching of Psychology, 10*(4), 234-236.

93. Colker, R., & Widom, C. (1980). Correlates of female athletic participation: Masculinity, femininity, self-esteem, and attitudes toward women. *Sex Roles: A Journal of Research, 6,* 47-58.

94. Committee on Scientific Awards. (1986). Distinguished scientific contributions. *American Psychologist, 41,* 337-354.

95. Constantinople, A. (1973). Masculinity-femininity: An exception to a famous dictum? *Psychological Bulletin, 80,* 389-407.

96. Cotera, M. (1980). Feminism: The Chicana and Anglo versions. A historical analysis. In M. B. Melville (Ed.), *Twice a minority. Mexican American women.* St. Louis: C.V. Mosby.

97. Cox, C. L., & Glick, W. H. (1986). Resume evaluation and cosmetic use: When more is not better. *Sex Roles, 14*(1/2), 51-58.

98. Crandall, V. C. (1975) Sex differences in expectation of intellectual and academic reinforcement. In R. Unger & F.

Denmark (Eds.), *Woman: Dependent or independent variable?*
(pp. 650-685). New York: Psychological Dimensions.
Over various ages, girls and women consistently
underestimate their performance, based on their capabilities
and past performance.

99. Cronbach, L. (1970). *Essentials of psychological testing.*
New York: Harper & Row.
The bandwidth vs. fidelity dilemma is discussed.

100. Cronbach, L., Gleser, G., & Nanda, H. (1972). *The
dependability of behavioral measurements.* New York: Wiley.
A highly technical book which discusses in depth
generalizability of scores, and definition of individual
differences as measurable quantities or errors of
measurement.

101. Crovitz, E., & Buford, E. (1978). *Courage knows no sex.*
North Quincy, MA: Christopher Publishing House.

102. Dalton, K. (1960). Schoolgirl's misbehavior and menstruation.
British Medical Journal, 2, 1647-1649.
British schoolgirls tend to break more rules and
consequently receive more punishment during certain phases
of their menstrual cycle. An interaction between both
hormonal influences and societal reactions to girls'
aggressions is demonstrated.

103. Dan, A. J., & Beekman, S. (1972). Male versus female
representation in psychological research. *American
Psychologist, 27,* 1078.

104. Dan, A. J., Graham, E. A., & Bucher, C. P. (1980). *The
menstrual cycle Vol. 1.* New York: Springer.

105. Danziger, K. (1985). The origins of the psychological
experiment as social institution. *American Psychologist, 40,*
133-140.

106. Deaux, K. (1976). *The behavior of women and men.*
Monterey, CA: Brooks/Cole.
Covers many traditional areas of social psychology from a
feminist perspective. Includes: stereotypes of women and
men, achievement motivation, verbal and nonverbal
communication, altruism, aggression, cooperation, group
behavior, interpersonal attraction.

107. ——. (1985). Sex and gender. *Annual Review of Psychology, 36*, 49-81.

108. Delaney, J., Lupton, M. J., & Toth, E. (1987). *The curse: A cultural history of menstruation.* Chicago, IL: University of Illinois Press.

109. Denes, M. (1977). *In necessity and sorrow.* New York: Penguin.

110. Denmark, F. L. (1980). Psyche: From rocking the cradle to rocking the boat. *American Psychologist, 35,* 1957-2065.

111. ——. (1983). Integrating the psychology of women into introductory psychology. In C. J. Scheirer & A. Rogers (Eds.), *The G. Stanley Hall Lecture Series,* (Vol. 3., pp. 22-75). Washington, DC: American Psychological Association.

112. Denmark, F. L., & Goodfield, H. M. (1978). A second look at adolescence theories. *Sex Roles, 4,* 375-80.
Examination of the double-bind in the lives of young women.

113. Dilling, C., & Claster, B. (Eds.). (1985). *Female psychology: A partially annotated bibliography.* New York: New York City Coalition for Women's Mental Health.
Useful resource to introduce students to the literature as they develop research projects.

114. Doherty, M. A. (1973). Sexual bias in personality theory. *Counseling Psychologist, 4*(1), 67-74.

115. Donnerstein, E. (1980). Pornography and violence against women: Experimental studies. *Annals of the New York Academy of Sciences, 347,* 277-288.
Research examining the effects of media presentations on aggression against women.

116. Downing, M. (1974). Heroines of the daytime serial. *Journal of Communication, 24,* 130-137.
Critique of the role of women as presented in T.V. characters.

117. Dunlop, K. H. (1981). Maternal employment and child care. *Professional Psychology, 12,* 67-75.

118. Dweck, C. S., Davidson, W., Nelson, S., & Enna, B. (1978). Sex differences in learned helplessness: The contingencies of

evaluative feedback in the classroom; An experimental analysis. *Developmental Psychology, 14*(3), 268-276.

119. Eagly, A. H. (1978). Sex differences in influenceability. *Psychological Bulletin, 85*, 86-116.
     Examines the hypothesis that women are more influenceable than men.

120. Eberts, C. G., & Gray, P. H. (1982). Evaluating the historical treatment of female psychologists of distinction using citation analysis and textbook coverage. *Bulletin of the Psychonomic Society, 20*, 7-10.

121. Ehrenreich, B., & English, D. (1978). *For her own good: 150 years of the experts' advice to women.* Garden City, NY: Anchor Press/ Doubleday.

122. Eron, L. (1981). Prescription for reduction of aggression. *American Psychologist, 35*, 244-252.
     Eron suggests that if males' socialization were more similar to females', expression of aggression would be reduced.

123. Escamilla-Mondanaro, J. (1977). Lesbians and therapy. In E. Rawlings & D. Carter (Eds.), *Psychotherapy for women: Treatment toward equality* (pp. 256-265). Springfield, IL: Charles C. Thomas.

124. Espin, O., & Lovelace, V. (1981). A brief annotated bibliography on third world women: Resources for mental health practitioners (1955-1980). *JSAS Catalog of Selected Documents in Psychology, 11*, 70.
     A useful resource to introduce students to literature on ethnic minority women.

125. Farina, A., & Fisher, J. D. (1982). Beliefs about mental disorders. In G. Weary & H. F. Mirels (Eds.), *Integrations of clinical and social psychology* (pp. 48-71). New York: Oxford University Press.

126. Fausto-Sterling, A. (1985). *Myths of gender: Biological theories about women and men.* New York: Basic Books.

127. Fee, E. (1983). Women's nature and scientific objectivity. In M. Lowe & R. Hubbard (Eds.), *Woman's nature: Rationalizations of inequality* (pp. 9-28). Elmsford, NY: Pergamon Press.

128. Feil, R. N., Largey, G. P., & Miller, M. (1984). Attitudes toward abortion as a means of sex selection. *Journal of Psychology, 116*, 269-272.

129. Fein, J. (1981). *Are you a target?* Belmont, CA: Wadsworth, 1981.

130. Fein, R. A. (1978). Research on fathering: Social policy and an emergent perspective. *Journal of Social Issues, 34*(1), 122-135.

131. Fennema, E., & Sherman, J. (1977). Sex-related differences in mathematics achievement, spatial visualization and affective factors. *American Educational Research Journal, 4*, 51-71.
     Controlling for spatial ability eliminates sex differences in math achievement.

132. Fidell, L. (1981). Sex differences in psychotropic drug use. *Professional Psychology, 12*, 156-162.

133. Fidell, L., Hoffman, D., & Keith-Spiegel, P. (1979). Some social implications of sex-choice technology. *Psychology of Women Quarterly, 4*, 32-42.

134. Fine, M., & Asch, A. (1981). Disabled women: Sexism without the pedestal. *Journal of Sociology and Social Welfare, 8*, 233-248.

135. Ford, M. R., & Lowery, C. R. (1986). Gender differences in moral reasoning: A comparison of the use of justice and care orientations. *Journal of Personality and Social Psychology, 50*, 777-783.

136. Frankel, M. T., & Rollins, H. A. (1983). Does mother know best? Mothers and fathers interacting with preschool sons and daughters. *Developmental Psychology, 19*, 694-702.

137. Franken, R. E. (1982). *Human motivation.* Monterey, CA: Brooks/Cole.
     A text which looks at the biological and social components of motivation. Six chapters concentrating on physiological drives are followed by chapters on stress, addiction, aggression and compliance, controllability, helplessness, achievement, persistence and endurance, consciousness, curiosity and competence, altruism, and work motivation.

Women's issues are given an even-handed treatment
throughout.

138. Franks, V., & Burtle, V. (Eds.). (1974). *Women in therapy:
New psychotherapies for a changing society.* New York:
Brunner/Mazel.
An examination of how feminism has affected the practices
of mental health professionals, with a focus on treatment of
female phobias, depression, alcoholism, homosexuality, and
experiences in mental hospitals.

139. Franks, V., & Rothblum, E. (Eds.). (1983). *The stereotyping
of women: Its effects on mental health.* New York:
Springer.
The contributions of sex role stereotypes to the prevalence
of female depression, agoraphobia, and sexual dysfunction
are considered. Special issues of living for women which
lead to obesity and lack of assertiveness are discussed.

140. Frazier, N., & Sadker, M. (1973). *Sexism in school and
society.* New York: Harper and Row.

141. Freed, N. (1983). Prospective mathematical equivalence by
gender: Still more inadvertent support. *Psychological
Reports, 53,* 677-678.

142. Freedman, R. (1986). *Beauty bound.* Lexington, MA:
Lexington Books.

143. ———. (1984). Reflections on beauty as it relates to health
in adolescent females. In S. Golub (Ed.), *Health care of the
female adolescent* (pp. 29-46). New York: Haworth Press.

144. Freedman, R., Golub, S., & Krauss, B. (1982). Mainstreaming
the psychology of women into the core curriculum.
Teaching of Psychology, 9, 165-168.

145. Frieze, I., Parsons, J., Johnson, P., Ruble, D., & Zellman, G.
(1978). *Women and sex roles: A social psychological
perspective.* New York: Norton.
A good resource for materials on sexism in the methodology
of psychological research.

146. Frodi, A., Macaulay, J., & Thorne, P. R. (1977). Are women
always less aggressive than men? A review of the
experimental literature. *Psychological Bulletin, 84,* 634-660.

147. Furumoto, L. (1986). Placing women in the history of
     psychology course. *Teaching of Psychology, 12*(4), 203-206.

148. Furumoto, L., & Scarborough, E. (1986). Placing women in
     the history of psychology: The first generation of American
     women psychologists. *American Psychologist, 41*(1), 35-42.

149. Garai, J. E., & Scheinfeld, A. (1968). Sex differences in
     mental and behavioral traits. *Genetic Psychology
     Monographs, 17,* 169-299.

150. Garner, D., & Garfinkel, P., et al. (1980). Cultural
     expectations of thinness in women. *Psychological Reports,
     47*(2).

151. Garza, R., & Lipton, J. (1978). Culture, personality and
     reactions to praise and criticism. *Journal of Personality, 46,*
     743-761.
     Male and female reactions to praise and criticism differed
     between the sexes and in Anglo-American and Mexican-
     American subcultures.

152. Gelles, R. (1974). *The violent home: A study of physical
     aggression between husbands and wives.* New York: Sage.

153. Gelles, R., & Pedrick-Cornell, C. (1981). Watch on the right:
     Beware the "Research Shows" ploy. *Ms.,* June, 100.

154. Gerson, M., Alper, J. L., & Richardson, M. S. (1984).
     Mothering: The view from psychological research. *Signs, 9,*
     434-453.

155. Gilbert, L. (1980). Feminist therapy. In A. Brodsky & R.
     Hare-Mustin (Eds.), *Women and psychotherapy* (pp. 245-266).
     New York: Guilford.

156. Gilligan, C. (1977). In a different voice: Women's
     conceptions of the self and morality. *Harvard Educational
     Review, 47,* 481-517.
     The process of making an abortion decision is viewed from a
     feminist conception of moral development.

157. ———. (1982). *In a different voice.* Cambridge, MA:
     Harvard University Press.

158. Gladding, S. T., & Huber, C. H. (1984). The position of the single-parent father. *Journal of Employment Counseling, 21,* 13-18.

159. Goldberg, P. (1968). Are women prejudiced against women? *Trans-Action,* April, 28-30.

160. Golden, M. P. (Ed.). (1976). *The research experience.* Itasca, IL: F. E. Peacock.

161. Goldstein, E. (1979). Effect of same-sex and cross-sex role models on the subsequent academic productivity of scholars. *American Psychologist, 34,* 407-410.

162. Goldstein, K., & Blackman, S. (1978). *Cognitive style.* New York: Wiley.
     Cognitive style is hypothesized to be a mediator between stimulus and response. Few, if any, sex differences in cognitive style are found in the literature that cannot be accounted for by differences in child rearing practices.

163. Golub, S. (1978). The decision to breast-feed: Personality and experiential influences *Psychology: A Journal of Human Behavior, 15,* 17-27.

164. ———. (1981). Sex differences in attitudes toward menstruation. In P. Kommenich, M. McSweeney, J. A. Noach, & Sr. N. Elder (Eds.) *The menstrual cycle Vol. 2* (pp. 237-246) New York: Springer.

165. ———. (Ed.). (1983). Lifting the curse of menstruation: A feminist appraisal of the influence of menstruation on women's lives. (Special issue) *Women and Health, 8,*(2,3). Addresses issues related to menstruation over the life cycle, from menarche to menopause, and includes discussion of dysmenorrhea, premenstrual syndrome, and research on the relationship between psychopathology and the menstrual cycle.

166. ———. (1985). The beginning of menstrual life. In J. Williams (Ed.), *Psychology of women: Selected readings* (pp. 95-109). New York: W. W. Norton.

167. Golub, S., & Canty, E. (1982). Sex role expectations and the assumption of leadership by college women. *Journal of Social Psychology, 116,* 83-90.

168. Gomberg, E. S. L. (1981). Women, sex roles, and alcohol problems. *Professional Psychology, 12,* 146-155.

169. Goodenough, D. R., & Witkin, H. A. (1977). *Origins of the field-dependent and field-independent cognitive styles.* Princeton, NJ: ETS.
Despite the literature to the contrary, the authors find no sex differences in field dependence-independence on the Embedded Figures Test and only a slight advantage to males on the Rod and Frame Test. Field-dependence correlates with an interpersonal orientation and psychological health.

170. Gordon, D. P. (1983). The influence of sex on the development of lateralization of speech. *Neuropsychologic, 21,* 139-146.

171. Gore, D. A., & Roumagoux, D. V. (1983). Wait - time as a variable in sex-related differences during fourth-grade mathematics instruction. *Journal of Educational Research, 76,* 273-275.

172. Gould, L. (1972, June). X: A fabulous child's story. *MS.*

173. Gould, S. J. (1981). *The mismeasure of man.* New York: W. W. Norton & Co.

174. Gove, W. R. (1979). Sex differences in the epidemiology of mental disorder: Explanation. In E. S. Gomberg & V. Franks (Eds.), *Gender and disorder behavior* (pp. 23-68). New York: Brunner/Mazel.

175. Gove, W., Hughes, M. & Style, C. (1983). Does marriage have positive effects on psychological well-being of the individual? *Journal of Health and Social Behavior, 24*(2), 122-131.

176. Goy, R. (1970). Early hormonal influences on the development of sexual and sex-related behavior. In F. Schmitt (Ed.), *The neuro-sciences: Second study program* (pp. 197-207). New York: Rockefeller University Press.
Documents that the relationship among hormones, physical structures, maturation, and behavior defy simple generalizations.

177. Goy, R. W., & McEwen, B. S. (1980). *Sexual differentiation of the brain.* Cambridge, MA: MIT Press.
A thorough treatment of brain organization and functional sex differences.

178. Grady, K. E. (1979). Androgyny reconsidered. In J. H. Williams (Ed.), *Psychology of women: Selected readings* (pp. 172-178). New York: W. W. Norton & Co.

179. ———. (1981). Sex bias in research design. *Psychology of Women Quarterly, 5,* 628-636.

180. Greenwald, A. G. (1975). Consequences of prejudice against the null hypothesis. *Psychological Bulletin, 82,* 1-20.

181. Grow, M. F., & Johnson, N. (1983). Math learning: The two hemispheres. *Journal of Humanistic Education and Development, 22,* 30-39.

182. Guthrie, R. V. (1976). *Even the rat was white.* New York: Harper & Row.

183. Hacker, H. M. (1975). Women as a minority group...and...women as a minority group twenty years later. In R. Unger & F. Denmark (Eds.), *Woman: Dependent or independent variable?* (pp. 86-115). New York: Psychological Dimensions.
A sociologist looks at the status of women in U. S. culture.

184. Hall, R. M., & Sandler, B. R. (1982). The classroom climate: A chilly one for women? Available from the Project on the Status and Education of Women, Association of American Colleges, 1818 R St., N.W., Washington, DC, 20009.

185. Hall, S. M., & Havassy, B. (1981). The obese woman: Causes, correlates, and treatment. *Professional Psychology, 12,* 163-170.

186. Hamilton, R. (1980). *The herpes book.* Boston: Houghton Mifflin Co.

187. Hare-Mustin, R. T., & Broderick, P. C. (1979). The myth of motherhood: A study of attitudes toward motherhood. *Psychology of Women Quarterly, 4,* 114-128.

188. Hariton, B. E. (1973). The sexual fantasies of women. *Psychology Today, 6*(10), 39-44.

189. Harmon, L. (1973). Sex bias in interest measurement. *Measurement and Evaluation in Guidance, 5,* 496-501.

190. Harway, M., & Astin, H. S. (1977). *Sex discrimination in career counseling and education.* New York: Praeger. A complete detailed overview of sex bias in career counseling, vocational tests, and counselor interaction with female students.

191. Hastrup, K. (1978). The semantics of biology: Virginity. In S. Ardener (Ed.), *Defining females* (pp. 49-65). New York: Halstead Press. Cultural definitions of virginity and its meaning for women's lives.

192. Haug, M. R., Ford, A. B., & Sheafor, M. (1985). *The physical and mental health of aged women.* New York: Springer. Provides an interdisciplinary perspective on physical and mental health issues for aging women, including depression, grief, poverty, institutionalization, and rehabilitation.

193. Heiman, J. R. (1975). The physiology of erotica: Women's sexual arousal. *Psychology Today, 8,*(11), 90-94.

194. Helson, R. (1967). Sex differences in creative style. *Journal of Personality, 35,* 214-233. Examines the matriarchal (brooding, summarizing, realizing) and patriarchal (purposeful, assertive, objective) styles of 90 male and female mathematicians.

195. Henley, N., & Thorne, B. (1977). Womanspeak and manspeak: Sex differences and sexism in communication, verbal and nonverbal. In A. G. Sargent (Ed.), *Beyond sex roles* (pp. 201-218). New York: West Publishing Co.

196. Herman, D. (1984). The rape culture. In J. Freeman (Ed.), *Women: A feminist perspective* (pp. 20-38). Palo Alto, CA: Mayfield.

197. Herman, J. (1981a). Father-daughter incest. *Professional Psychology, 12,* 76-80.

198. ———. (1981b). *Father-daughter incest.* Cambridge, MA: Harvard Univ. Press.

199. Hetherington, E. M. (1972). Effects of father absence on personality development in adolescent daughters. *Developmental Psychology, 7*, 313-326.

200. Hilberman, E. (1976). *The rape victim.* Washington, DC: American Psychiatric Association.

201. Hite, S. (1976). *The Hite report.* New York: MacMillan.

202. ———. (1981). *The Hite report on male sexuality.* New York: Knopf.

203. Hoffman, L. W., & Maier, N. R. F. (1966). Social factors influencing problem solving in women. *Journal of Personality and Social Psychology, 4,* 382-390.

204. Hoffman, L. W. (1974). Effects of maternal employment on the child: A review of the research. *Developmental Psychology, 10,* 204-228.

205. ———. (1979). Maternal employment: 1979. *American Psychologist, 34,* 859-865.

206. ———. (1980). The effects of maternal employment on the academic attitudes and performance of school aged children. *School Psychology Review, 9,* 319-335.

207. Hoffnung, M. (1986). Feminist transformations: Teaching experimental psychology. *Feminist Teacher, 2,* 31-35.

208. Horner, M. (1970). Femininity and successful achievement: A basic inconsistency. In J. M. Bardwick, E. Douvan, M. S. Horner & D. Gutmann, *Feminine personality and conflict* (pp. 45-76). Belmont, CA: Brooks/Cole.

209. ———. (1972). Toward an understanding of achievement related conflicts in women. *Journal of Social Issues, 28,* 157-175.
Hypothesis that successful achievement often leads to negative consequences for women, inducing a fear of success.

210. How to cope with herpes. Pamphlet available from American Social Health Association, 260 Sheridan Ave. Palo Alto, CA, 94306.

211. Howell, E., & Bayes, M. (Eds.). (1981). *Women and mental health.* New York: Basic Books.
Includes some of the best of the psychodynamic writings on women plus information on special concerns of women such as: incest, rape, female addiction, teenage pregnancy, and wife beating.

212. Hubbard, R., & Lowe, M. (Eds.). (1979). *Genes and gender: II. Pitfalls in research on sex and gender.* New York: Gordian Press.

213. Huston-Stein, A., & Higgen-Trenk, A. (1978). Development of females from childhood through adulthood: Career and feminine role orientation. In P. Battes (Ed.), *Life span development and behavior (Vol. 1)* (pp. 258-297). New York: Academic Press.

214. Hyde, J. S. (1981). How large are cognitive gender differences? *American Psychologist, 36*(8), 892-901.
Hyde reanalyzes the data used to establish gender differences in verbal, quantitative, and spatial ability. She notes the magnitude of such differences is not large. However, the variability is such that it is difficult to justify making selection decisions on the basis of gender.

215. ———. (1984). Children's understanding of sexist language. *Developmental Psychology, 20*, 697-706.

216. ———. (1985a). *Half the human experience: The psychology of women.* Lexington, MA: Heath.

217. ———. (1985b). *Understanding human sexuality.* New York: McGraw-Hill.

218. Hyde, J. S., Rosenberg, B. G., & Behrman, J. (1977). Tomboyism. *Psychology of Women Quarterly, 2*, 73-75.

219. Iversen, I., Silberberg, N., & Silberberg, M. (1970). Sex differences in knowledge of letter and number names in kindergarten. *Perceptual and Motor Skills, 31*, 79-85.
The author's note, albeit with a sample of less than 50 males and less than 50 females, that a higher percentage of boys than girls enter kindergarten knowing eight or more number names while girls tend to know more letter names.

220. Jackaway, R., & Teevan, R. (1976). Fear of failure and fear of success: Two dimensions of the same motive. *Sex Roles, 2*, 283-294.

221. Jacklin, C. N. (1979). Epilogue. In M. A. Wittig & A. C. Petersen (Eds.), *Sex-related differences in cognitive functioning* (pp. 331-371). New York. Academic Press.

222. Jacklin, C. N., DiPietro, J. A., & Maccoby, E. E. (1984). Sex-typing behavior and sex-typing pressure in child/parent interaction. *Archives of Sexual Behavior, 13*, 413-425.

223. Jamison, P. H., Franzini, L. R., & Kaplan, R. M. (1979). Some assumed characteristics of voluntarily childfree women and men. *Psychology of Women Quarterly, 4*, 266-273.

224. Jarett, L. R., & Everhart, D. (1983). Effect of sex of patient and clinician on mental status descriptions of attractiveness. *Psychotherapy: Theory, Research and Practice, 20*(4), 468-475.

225. Jeffries, D., (1976). Counseling for the strengths of black women. *The Counseling Psychologist, 7*, 20-22.
Strengths of black women are used as a starting point for the development of counseling theory. The history of the role of black women in the workplace is traced and data which support the egalitarianism of black families are provided.

226. Johnson, M., & Auerbach, R. H. (1984). Women and psychotherapy research. In L. E. Walker (Ed.), *Women and mental health policy* (pp. 59-78). Beverly Hills, CA: Sage.

227. Jones, C., & Aronson, E. (1973). Attribution of fault to a rape victim as a function of respectability of the victim. *Journal of Personality and Social Psychology, 26*, 415-419.

228. Jones, L. M., & McBride, J. L. (1980). Sex-role stereotyping in children as a function of maternal employment. *Journal of Social Psychology, 111*, 219-223.

229. Kahn, A. (Ed.). (1984). *Social psychology.* Dubuque, IA: W. C. Brown.

230. Kahn, A. S., & Jean, P. J. (1983). Integration and elimination or separation and redefinition: The future of the psychology of women. *Signs: Journal of Women in Culture and Society, 8*, 659-671.

231. Kahn, S. E., & Theurer, G. (in press). Graduate education and evaluation in counseling women: A case study. In L. B. Rosewater & L. E. Walker (Eds.), *A Handbook of feminist therapy: Women's issues in psychotherapy.* New York: Springer.

232. Kanter, R. M. (1977). Women in organizations: Sex roles, group dynamics, and change strategies. In A. G. Sargent (Ed.), *Beyond sex roles* (pp. 371-386). New York: West Publishing Co.
     Group behavior, women and leadership, stereotypical roles assumed by women in organizations, job segregation with respect to sex, and change strategies.

233. Kaplan, A., & Sedney, M. A. (1980). *Psychology of sex roles.* Boston, MA: Little, Brown Co.

234. Kaplan, M. (1983). A woman's view of DSM-III: Comments on the articles by Spitzer, Williams, and Kass. *American Psychologist, 38*(7), 799-801.

235. Kaschak, E. (1981). Feminist psychotherapy: The first decade. In S. Cox (Ed.), *Female psychology: The emerging self.* New York: St. Martin's Press.

236. Katz, P. A. (1979). The development of female identity. *Sex Roles, 5*(2), 155-178.

237. Kedar-Viovodas, G. (1983). The impact of elementary school children's school roles and sex roles on teacher attitudes: An interactional analysis. *Review of Educational Research, 53*, 415-437.

238. Keller, E. F. (1985). *Reflections on gender and science.* New Haven: Yale University Press.

239. Kessler, S. J., & McKenna, W. (1978). *Gender: An ethnomethodological approach.* New York: John Wiley & Sons.

240. Kieffer, C. H. (1984). Citizen empowerment: A developmental perspective. *Studies in empowerment: Steps toward*

understanding and action (pp. 9-36). New York: The
Haworth Press.
[Also published as *Prevention in Human Services*, (Volume 3,
Nos. 2/3).]

241. Kilmann, P. R., & Mills, K. II. (1983). *All about sex therapy*
New York: Plenum.

242. Kimble, G. A. (1984). Psychology's two cultures. *American
Psychologist, 39*, 833-839.
See also rejoinder by R. K. Unger (1985). Epistemological
consistency and its scientific implications, *American
Psychologist, 40*, 1413-1414; and rejoinder by S. B. Messer
(1985), Choice of method is value laden too. *American
Psychologist, 40*, 1414-1415.

243. Kinsey, A. C., Pomeroy, W. B., Martin, C. E., & Gebhard, P.
H. (1953). *Sexual behavior in the human female.*
Philadelphia: Saunders.

244. Kolata, G. B. (1979). Scientists attack report that
obstetrical medications endanger children. *Science, 204*,
391-392.

245. Kolbe, R., & LaVoie, J. C. (1981). Sex-role stereotyping in
preschool children's picture books. *Social Psychology
Quarterly, 44*, 369-374.

246. Kravetz, D., Marecek, J., & Finn, S. E. (1983). Factors
influencing women's participation in consciousness-raising
groups. *Psychology of Women Quarterly, 7*(3), 257-271.

247. Krieger, S. (1983). *The mirror dance: Identity in a women's
community.* Philadelphia, PA: Temple University Press.
Describes women's struggles for identity in gay community
in the Midwest.

248. Kushner, R. (1975). *Breast cancer: A personal history and
an investigative report.* New York: Harcourt Brace
Jovanovich.

249. Lagone, J., & Lagone, D. (1980). *Women who drink.*
Reading, MA: Addison-Wesley.
An introduction to the varied aspects of women's relations
to alcohol. Discusses stereotypes about alcohol consumption
by women, theories about why women drink and become
alcoholic, the effects of drinking upon the woman herself

and upon her husband and children, how others innocently "protect" women from getting the help they need, and resources for helping women with drinking problems.

250. Lakoff, R. (1975). *Language and woman's place.* New York: Harper Colophon Books.
A short book describing the way in which language both reflects and influences our perception of self and others. Explains what "talking like a lady" means.

251. Lamb, M. E. (1981). The development of father-infant relationships. In M. E. Lamb (Ed.), *The role of the father in child development.* New York: Wiley.

252. ———. (Ed.). (1982). *Nontraditional families: Parenting and child development.* Hillsdale, NJ: Lawrence Erlbaum.

253. Lamb, M. E., Owen, M. T., & Chase-Lansdale, L. (1979). The father-daughter relationship: Past, present and future. In C. B. Kopp (Ed.), *Becoming female: Perspectives on development* (pp. 89-112). New York: Plenum.

254. Langlois, J. H., & Downs, A. C. (1980). Mothers, fathers, and peers as socialization agents of sex-typed play behaviors in young children. *Child Development, 51,* 1237-1247.

255. Larin, H. M. (1982). Drug and obstetric medication effects on infant behavior as measured by the Brazelton Neonatal Behavioral Assessment Scale. *Physical & Occupational Therapy in Pediatrics, 2,* 75-84.

256. Laws, J. L., & Schwarz, P. (1977). *Sexual scripts: The social construction of female sexuality.* Hinsdale, IL: Dryden Press.
Female sexuality from a feminist perspective. Note particularly chapters on sexual transactions (dating, courtship), sexual life styles, and women as sexual criminals and victims.

257. Lee, P., & Stewart, R. (Eds.). (1976). *Sex differences: Cultural and developmental dimensions.* New York: Urizen Books.

258. Lerner, G. (1979). *The majority finds its past: Placing women in history.* New York: Oxford University Press.

259. Lerner, H. E. (1982). Special issues for women in psychotherapy. In M. T. Notman & C. C. Nadelson (Eds.), *The woman patient: Vol. 3. Aggression, adaptations and psychotherapy* (pp. 273-286). New York: Plenum.

260. ———. (1984a) *Bibliography on sexual intimacies between psychotherapist and patients.* Available from P. Hannigan, 120 Newport Centre Drive #200, Newport Beach, CA 92660 - $10.50 per copy.

261. ———. (1984b). Early origins of envy and devaluation of women: Implications for sex-role stereotypes. In P. P. Rieker & E. Carmen (Eds.), *The gender gap in psychotherapy: Social realities and psychological processes* (pp. 111-124). New York: Plenum.

262. Levekron, S. (1978). *The best little girl in the world.* New York: Contemporary Books. Anorexia, its origins and treatment approaches.

263. Levy, S. (1981). The aging woman: Developmental issues and mental health needs. *Professional Psychology, 12,* 92-102.

264. Lewin, M. (1984). *In the shadow of the past: Psychology portrays the sexes.* New York: Columbia University Press.

265. Liebmann-Smith, R. (1985). *The question of aids.* New York: New York Academy of Science.

266. Liss-Livenson, N., et. al. (1985). *Women and psychotherapy: A consumer handbook.* Tempe, AZ: National coalition for Women's Mental Health.

267. Lott, B. (1981). *Becoming a woman.* Springfield, IL: Charles Thomas.

268. ———. (1985). The potential enrichment of social/personality psychology through feminist research and vice versa. *American Psychologist, 40,* 155-164.

269. Maccoby, E. E. (1966). Sex differences in intellectual functioning. In E. Maccoby (Ed.), *The development of sex differences.* Stanford: Stanford University Press.

270. Maccoby, E. E., & Jacklin, C. N. (1971). Sex differences and their implications for sex roles. Paper presented at the 79th meeting of APA, Washington, D. C., September, 1971.

The emergence of sex-typed behavior is examined. Criteria for inferring true sex differences are specified.

271. ———. (1974a). Myth, reality and shades of gray: What we know and don't know about sex differences. *Psychology Today, 8*, 109-112.
Aggression appears to be one area in which "true" sex differences appear. Mathematical ability is a gray area. Many other hypothesized areas of difference have little empirical support.

272. ———. (1974b). *The psychology of sex differences. Vols. I and II.* Stanford: Stanford University Press.
Treats intelligence and achievement including perception, learning, memory, intellectual abilities, cognitive styles, achievement motives, and cognitive styles. "Studies of learning have dealt primarily with the learning process itself, and only tangentially with individual differences in how learning takes place or what is most easily learned." Vol. II is an annotated bibliography, an invaluable resource.

273. MacKinnon, D. W. (1975). IPAR's contribution to the conceptualization and study of creativity. In I. Taylor & J. Getzels (Eds.), *Perspectives in creativity* (pp. 60-89). Chigago: Aldine.
Traces the history of research on creativity in women with emphasis on Helson's work. Examines situational and personality factors which lead women's original contributions in arts, business, and science to be less than men's.

274. Magrab, P. (1979). Mothers and daughters. In C. B. Kopp (Ed.), *Becoming female: Perspectives on development* (pp. 113-129). New York: Plenum.

275. Maier, N. R. F., & Casselman, G. C. (1970). The SAT as a measure of problem-solving ability in males and females. *Psychological Reports, 26*, 927-939.
Notes the persistence of differences in problem-solving skill of men and women under conditions of matched ability.

276. Marecek, J., & Ballou, D. J. (1981). Family roles and women's mental health. *Professional Psychology, 12*, 39-46.

277. Markle, G. E., & Nam, C. B. (1983). Sex predetermination: Its impact on fertility. *Social Biology, 29*, 168-179.

278. Martin, C. L., & Halverson, C. F. (1981). A schematic processing model of sextyping and stereotyping in children. *Child Development, 52,* 1119-1134.

279. Martin, D. (1976). *Battered wives.* San Francisco: Glide Publications.
Portrays the victimization of physically abused wives and unmarried women who live with violent men, and provides extensive documentation on how traditional societal institutions fail to meet the needs of abused women.

280. ———. (1979). Battered wives. In A. Pines & C. Maslach (Eds.), *Experiencing social psychology* (pp. 118-128).
A look at the relationship between intimacy and aggression. The incidence of wife abuse and attitudes that sanction it.

281. Martin, D., & Lyon, P. (1984). Lesbian women and mental health policy. In L. E. Walker (Ed.), *Women and mental health policy.* Beverly Hills, CA: Sage.

282. Martin, J. R. (1985). *Reclaiming a conversation: The ideal of the educated woman.* New Haven, CT: Yale University Press.

283. Maslach, C., & Pines, A. (1979). Burnout: The loss of human caring. In A. Pines and C. Maslach (Eds.), *Experiencing social psychology* (pp. 246-252). New York: Knopf.
A look at the emotional burnout in the helping professions: nursing, social work, counseling, among others. Are women more susceptible?.

284. Masson, J. (1983). *The assault on truth: Freud's suppression of the seduction theory.* New York: Farrar, Strouse & Giroux, Inc.

285. Masters, W. H., & Johnson, V. (1966). *Human sexual response.* Boston: Little Brown.

286. Matthews, S. (1979). *The social world of old women: Management of self-identity.* Beverly Hills, CA: Sage.
Strategies widows use to avoid negative definitions of self are discussed. The relationship between stereotypes of the aged as sick, poor, and isolated and societal arrangements that perpetuate the marginal position of old people, especially women, is examined.

287. McHugh, M., Koeske, R., & Frieze, I. (1986). Issues to consider in conducting nonsexist research: A guide for researchers. *American Pyschologist, 41*, 879-890.

288. Mead, M. (1935). *Sex and temperament in three primitive societies.* New York: Morrow.

289. Messick, S. (1980). Test validity and the ethics of assessment. *American Psychologist, 35*, 1012-1027. A philosophical and sensitive treatment of the difference between the acquisition of psychological knowledge and the ethics of its use.

290. Miller, J. B. (Ed.). (1973). *Psychoanalysis and women.* Baltimore: Penguin Books.

291. ———. (1981). Intimacy: Its relation to work and family. *Journal of Psychiatric Treatment and Evaluation, 3*(2), 121-129.

292. Mitchell, J. (1974). *Psychoanalysis and feminism: Freud, Reich, Laing and women.* New York: Vintage Books.

293. Money, J., & Ehrhardt, A. (1972). *Man and woman: Boy and girl.* Baltimore: John Hopkins. The first chapters explore the social and biological determinants of gender identification. Common conceptions of sex as a simple dichotomy, male or female, are shown to be untenable by certain criteria.

294. Montrose, M. (1978, May). New options in childbirth, Part I: Family-centered maternity care. *American Baby,* pp. 52-54.

295. Mora, M., & Del Castillo, A. R. (Eds.). (1980). *Mexican women in the United States: Struggles past and present.* Los Angeles: UCLA Chicano Studies Research Center Publications.

296. Moreland, J., & Schwebel, A. I. (1981). A gender role transcendent perspective on fathering. *Counseling Psychologist, 9*, 45-53.

297. Morgan, R., & Steinem, G. (1980, March). The international crime of genital mutilation. *MS,* pp. 65-69, 98.

298. Myers, B. J. (1984). Mother-infant bonding: The status of this critical period hypothesis. *Developmental Review, 4,* 240-274.

299. Nadelson, C. C., & Notman, M. T. (1984). Reproductive advancements: Theory, research applications, and psychological issues. In L. E. Walker (Ed.), *Women and mental health policy* (pp. 117-134). Beverly Hills, CA: Sage.

300. Naditch, S. (1976). Sex differences in field dependence: The role of social influence. In *Determinants of gender differences in cognitive functioning.* Symposium presented at the American Psychological Association, Washington, D. C. Sex differences in the Rod and Frame Test disappear when the task is given a masculine orientation for males and a feminine orientation for females.

301. Newman, L. M. (1985). *Men's ideas/ women's realities: Popular science, 1870-1915.* New York: Pergamon Press.

302. Nicholls, J. G. (1975). Causal attributions and other achievement-related cognitions: Effects of task outcome, attainment value and sex. *Journal of Personality and Social Psychology, 31,* 379-389.
Females had self derogatory reactions to lack of success in an angle matching task, while males did not.

303. Nilson, A. P. (1977). Alternatives to sexist practices in the classroom. *Young Children, 32,* 53-58.

304. Notman, M. T., & Nadelson, C. C. (1982). *The woman patient: Vol. 3.* Aggression, adaptations and psychotherapy. New York: Plenum.

305. Novara, R. (1984). Women and mental health: A community viewpoint. *Women and Therapy, 3(3/4),* 57-62.

306. O'Connell, A., & Russo, N. F. (Eds.). (1983). *Models of achievement: Reflections of eminent women in psychology.* New York: Columbia University Press.

307. O'Leary, V. E. (1974). Some attitudinal barriers to occupational aspirations in women. *Psychological Bulletin, 81,* 809-826.
Reviews external factors, such as sex role stereotypes and attitudes toward competency in women, as well as internal

factors, such as fear of failure, low self-esteem, and role conflict, which may serve as barriers for women at work.

308. Olmedo, E. L., & Parron, D. L. (1981). Mental health of minority women: Some special issues. *Professional Psychology, 12,* 103-111.

309. Orbach, S. (1980). *Fat is a feminist issue: The anti-diet guide to permanent weight loss.* New York: Berkley Books.

310. ———. (1982). *Fat is a feminist issue-II: A program to conquer compulsive eating.* New York: Berkley Books.

311. Parlee, M. B. (1972). Comments on "Roles of activation and inhibition in sex differences in cognitive abilities." *Psychological Review, 79*(2), 180-184.
Exposes untested assumptions of Broverman, et al.

312. ———. (1975). Psychology: Review essay. *Signs: A Journal of Women in Culture and Society, 1,* 119-138.

313. ———. (1981). Appropriate control groups in feminist research. *Psychology of Women Quarterly, 5,* 637-644.

314. Parsons, J. E. (Ed.). (1980). *The psychobiology of sex differences and sex roles.* New York: Hemisphere.

315. Peplau, L. A. (1979). Power in dating relationships. In J. Freeman (Ed.), *Women: A feminist perspective* (pp. 106-121). Palo Alto, CA: Mayfield Pub. Co.
Examines both attitudes toward power and actual power relationships in traditional and liberal college couples.

316. Peplau, L. A., & Amaro, H. (1982). Understanding lesbian relationships. In W. Paul, J. D. Weinrich, J. C. Gonsiorek, & M. E. Hotwedt (Eds.), *Homosexuality: Social psychological and biological issues* (pp. 233-247). Beverly Hills, CA: Sage.

317. Peplau, L. A., & Gordon S. L. (1985). Women and men in love: Gender differences in close heterosexual relationships. In V. E. O'Leary, R. K. Unger, & B. S. Wallston (Eds.), *Women, gender, and social psychology* (pp. 257-291). Hillsdale, NJ: Erlbaum.

318. Perry, J. D., & Whipple, B. (1981). Pelvic muscle strength of female ejaculators: Evidence in support of a new theory of orgasm. *The Journal of Sex Research, 17,* 22-39.

319. Pharis, M. E., & Manosevitz, M. (1980). Parental models of infancy: A note on gender preferences for firstborns. *Psychological Reports, 47*, (3, Pt. 1) 763-768.

320. Pitcher, E., & Schultz, L. (1983) *Boys and girls at play.* New York: Praeger.

321. Plath, S. (1975). *The bell jar.* New York: Bantam Books. Fictional account of Plath's adolescent suicide attempt.

322. Pleck, J. H. (1975). Masculinity-femininity: Current and alternate paradigms. *Sex Roles, 1*, 111-178.

323. ———. (1976). The male sex role: Definitions, problems, and sources of change. *Journal of Social Issues, 32*, 155-164.

324. Pleck, J., & Sawyer, J. (Eds.). (1974). *Men and masculinity.* Englewood Cliffs, NJ: Prentice-Hall.

325. Polya, G. (1957). *How to solve it.* Garden City, NY: Doubleday.
The *classic* problem-solving book. Written by an eminent mathematician, it is simple and straightforward, a surprise to students who equate "arcane and muddled" with math. It includes advice to instructors on the classroom style that promotes thinking.

326. Porcino, J. (1983). *Growing older, getting better.* Reading, MA: Addison-Wesley.

327. Powell, G. J. (1979). Growing up black and female. In C. B. Kopp (Ed.), *Becoming female: Perspectives on development* (pp. 29-66). New York, Plenum.

328. *Psychology of Women Quarterly.* (1981). Special section of feminist research, *5*(4), 595-653.

329. Quina, K. (1986). Teaching research methods: A multidimensional feminist curricular transformation. Working paper No. 164. Available from Wellesley College Center for Research on Women. Wellesley, MA.

330. Rawlings, E. T., & Carter, D. K. (1977). Feminist and nonsexist psychotherapy. In E. I. Rawlings & D. Carter (Eds.), *Psychotherapy for women* (pp. 49-76). Springfield, IL: Charles C. Thomas.

331. Reinharz, S. (1984). *On Becoming a social scientist.* New Brunswick, NJ: Jossey-Bass, Inc.

332. Reykowski, J. (1982). Social motivation. *Annual Review of Psychology, 33,* 123-154.
Presents a synthesis of literature on the meaning of social others as goal objects.

333. Rich, A. (1976). *Of woman born.* New York: Norton.

334. Richardson, P. (1983). Women's perceptions of change in relationships shared with their husbands during pregnancy. *Maternal-Child Nursing Journal, 12,* 1-19.

335. Rickel, A. U., Gerrard, M., & Iscoe, I. (Eds.). (1984). *Social and psychological problems of women: Prevention and crisis intervention.* New York: Hemisphere Publishing.

336. Riger, S., & Galligan, P. (1980). Women in management: An exploration of competing paradigms. *American Psychologist, 35,* 902-910.

337. Robbins, J. H. (1982). Women's experience: Organizing a seminar on feminist therapy. *Women and Therapy, 1*(1), 45-54.

338. Roberts, H. (Ed.). (1981). *Doing feminist research.* London: Routledge & Kegan Paul.

339. Robson, K., & Moss, H. (1970). Patterns and determinants of maternal attachment. *Journal of Pediatrics, 77,* 976-985.

340. Rode, S., Change, P., Fisch, R., & Stroufe, L. (1981). Attachment patterns of infants separated at birth. *Developmental Psychology, 17,* 188-191.

341. Rodgers-Rose, L. (Ed.) (1980). *The black woman.* Beverly Hills, CA: Sage.
Includes research papers and theoretical essays by black women about black women that examine how they cope with various problems, their relationships with black men, their values, and their roles within the black family.

342. Rose, H., & Rose, S. (Eds.). (1976). *The radicalisation of science.* London: Macmillan.

343. Rose, S. (Ed.) (1986). *Advice for women scholars.* New York: Springer Publishers.

344. Rosenberg, F. R., & Simmons, G. (1975). Sex differences in the self-concept in adolescence. *Sex Roles, 1,* 147-159.

345. Rosenberg, R. (1982). *Beyond separate spheres : Intellectual roots of modern feminism.* New Haven, CT: Yale University Press.

346. Rosenfeld, S. (1980). Sex roles and societal reactions to mental illness. The labeling of "deviant" deviance. *Journal of Health and Social Behavior, 23,* 18-24.

347. Rosewater, L. B. (1984). Feminist therapy: Implications for practitioners. In L. E. Walker (Ed.), *Women and mental health policy.* Beverly Hills, CA: Sage.

348. Rossi, J. (1983). Ratios exaggerate gender differences in mathematical ability. *American Psychologist, 38,* 348-349.

349. Rossiter, M. W. (1982) *Women scientists in America: Struggles and strategies to 1940.* Baltimore, MD: Johns Hopkins University Press.

350. Roth, G. (1982). *Feeding the hungry heart: The experience of compulsive eating.* New York: Bobbs-Merrill.
Describes women's struggles with compulsive hungers.

351. Rothblum, E. D. (1983). Sex-role stereotypes and depression in women. In V. Franks & E. Rothblum (Eds.), *The stereotyping of women: Its effects on mental health* (pp. 83-111). New York: Springer.

352. Rothman, S. M. (1978). *Women's proper place: A history of changing ideals and practices, 1870 to the present.* New York: Basic Books, Inc.

353. Rubin, J. Z., Provenzano, F. J., & Luria, Z. (1985). The eye of the beholder: Parents' views on sex of newborns. In J. H. Williams (Ed.), *Psychology of women* (pp. 147-154). New York: W. W. Norton & Co.

354. Rubin, L. (1979). *Women of a certain age: The midlife search for self.* New York: Harper and Row.
Examines women's search for "a new identity not tied to mothering and homemaking" after their children leave home

and they must confront the unresolved problems of just who they are and how they will live the rest of their lives.

355. Rubin, Z. (1982). The love research. In D. Krebs (Ed.), *Readings in social psychology.* New York: Harper & Row.

356. Runyan, W. M. (1982). *Histories and psychobiography: Explorations in theory and methods.* New York: Oxford University Press.

357. Russo, N. F. (1979). Overview: Sex roles, fertility, and the motherhood mandate. *Psychology of Women Quarterly, 4,* 7-15.

358. ——. (Ed.). (1979 Fall). The motherhood mandate. *Psychology of Women Quarterly,* Whole No. 1.

359. ——. (1982). *Resources for teaching the history of women in psychology.* Office for Women's Programs, American Psychological Association, 1200 Seventeenth St. NW, Washington, DC 20036.

360. ——. (1984). Women in the mental health delivery system: Implications for research and public policy. In L. E. Walker (Ed.), *Women and Mental Health Policy* (pp. 21-42). Beverly Hills, CA: Sage.

361. ——. (Ed.). (1985a). *A women's mental health agenda.* Washington, DC: American Psychological Association.

362. ——. (1985b). Integrating information about the psychology of women into the teaching, research and practice of psychology: Developmental psychology. Published in *Proceedings of the XXIII International Congress of Psychology.* Amsterdam, The Netherlands: Elsevier Science Publishers.

363. Russo, N. F., & Denmark, F. L. (1984). Women, psychology, and public policy: Selected issues. *American Psychologist, 39,* 1161-1165.

364. Russo, N. F., & O'Connell, A. N. (1980). Models from our past: Psychology's foremothers. *Psychology of Women Quarterly, 5,* 11-54.

365. Russo, N. F. & Sobel, S. B. (1981). Sex differences in the utilization of mental health facilities. *Professional Psychology, 12,* 7-19.

366. Sales, E., & Frieze, I. H. (1984). Women and work: Implications for mental health. In L. E. Walker (Ed.), *Women and mental health policy* (pp. 229-246). Beverly Hills, CA: Sage.

367. Sandberg, E. C., & Jacobs, R. I. (1971). Psychology of the misuse and rejection of contraception. *American Journal of Obstetrics and Gynecology, 110,* 227-242.

368. Scarborough, E., & Furumoto, L. (1986). *American psychology's well kept secret: Women in the early period of the discipline.* New York: Columbia University Press.

369. Schau, C. G., & Scott, K. P. (1984). Impact of gender characteristics of instructional materials: An integration of the research literature. *Journal of Educational Psychology, 76,* 183-193.

370. Schusterman, L. (1985). The psychosocial factors of the abortion experience: A critical review. In J. Williams (Ed.), *Psychology of women: Selected readings* (pp. 353-375). New York: W. W. Norton.

371. Seavy, C., Katz, P., & Zik, S. (1975). Baby X: The effects of gender labels on adult responses to infants. *Sex Roles, 1,* 103-110.

372. Seligman, M. (1970). On the generality of the laws of learning. *Psychological Review, 77,* 406-418. The laws of learning may differ for contraprepared, prepared, and neutral responses.

373. Senn, M. L. (1975). Insights on the child development movement in the United States. *Monographs of the Society for Research in Child Development, 40*(3-4, Serial No. 16), 1-106.

374. Serbin, L. A., & O'Leary, K. D. (1979). How nursery schools teach girls to shut up. In J. H. Williams (Ed.), *Psychology of women* (pp. 183-187). New York: W. W. Norton & Co.

375. Sexton, V. S. (1974). Women in American psychology: An overview. *Journal of International Understanding, 9,* 66-77.

376. Sherman, J. (1976). Social values, femininity, and the
     development of female competence. *Journal of Social Issues,
     32*, 181-195.
     The goals of femininity and competence may not be the
     same. Suggests approaches to social change which may be
     fruitful.

377. ———. (1978). *Sex related differences in cognitive
     functioning.* Springfield, IL: Charles Thomas.
     Comprehensive overview of the nature and extent of sex
     differences in verbal, math, spatial and analytic abilities.
     Causative factors are analyzed.

378. ———. (1980). Therapist attitudes and sex-role stereotyping.
     In A. Brodsky & R. T. Hare-Mustin (Eds.), *Women and
     psychotherapy.* New York: Guilford Press.

379. ———. (1983). Factors predicting girls and boys enrollment
     in college preparatory mathematics. *Psychology of Women
     Quarterly, 7*, 272-281.

380. Shields, S. A. (1975a). Functionalism, Darwinism, and the
     psychology of women: A study in social myth. *American
     Psychologist, 30*, 739-754.

381. ———. (1975b). Ms. Pilgrim's progress: The contribution of
     Leta Stetter Hollingworth to the psychology of women.
     American Psychologist, 30, 852-857.

382. Shields, S., & Cooper, P. (1983) Stereotypes of traditional
     and nontraditional childbearing roles. *Sex Roles, 9*, 363-
     376.

383. Signorella, M. L., Begega, M. E., & Mitchell, M. E. (1981).
     Subject selection and analyses for sex-related differences:
     1968-70 and 1975-77. *American Psychologist, 36*, 988-990.

384. Smith, E. (1985). The black female adolescent. In J.
     Williams (Ed.), *Psychology of women: Selected readings* (pp.
     193-216). New York: W. W. Norton.

385. Smith, M. L. (1980). Sex bias in counseling and
     psychotherapy. *Psychological Bulletin, 392-407.*

386. Sobel, S. D., & Russo, N. F. (Eds.). (1981). Sex roles, equality, and mental health. Special issue of *Professional Psychology, 12.*
Includes many articles on relevant topics separately listed in this bibliography as well as articles that specifically focus on the role of the professional psychologist.

387. Solomon, B. M. (1985). *In the company of educated women: A history of women and higher education in America.* New Haven, CT: Yale University Press.

388. Sommer, B. (1973). The effect of menstruation on cognitive and perceptual-motor behavior: A review. *Psychosomatic Medicine, 35,* 515-534.

389. ———. (1984). The troubled teen: Suicide, drug use, and running away. In S. Golub (Ed.), *Health care of the female adolescent* (pp. 117-141). New York: Haworth Press.

390. Spence, J. T. (1982). Comments on Baumrind's "Are androgynous individuals more effective persons and parents?" *Child Development, 53,* 76-80.

391. Spouse Abuse, (Spring 1978). *Victimology: An International Journal.* (Special Issue).
The articles in this journal offer an indepth analysis of why family members commit violence against one another.

392. Springer, S. P., & Deutsch, G. (1981). *Left brain right brain.* San Francisco: W. H. Freeman.

393. St. Peter, S. (1979). Jack went up the hill...but where was Jill? *Psychology of Women Quarterly, 4,* 256-260.

394. Stanley, J. C., & Benbow, C. P. (1982). Huge sex ratios at upper end: Stanley and Benbow on Hyde. *American Psychologist, 37,* 972.
A reply to Hyde.

395. Steil, J. M. (1983). Marriage: An unequal partnership. In B. Wolman & G. Stricker (Eds.), *Handbook of family and marital therapy* (pp. 49-60). New York: Plenum.

396. Stein, A. H., & Bailey, M. M. (1973). The socialization of achievement orientation in females. *Psychological Bulletin, 80,* 345-365.

397. Steinbacker, R. (1980). Preselection of sex. *The Sciences,*
     April, 6.

398. Stephenson, S., & Walker, L. E. (1980). Psychotropic drugs
     and women. *Bioethics Quarterly, 2.*

399. Stevens, G., & Gardner, S. (1982). *The women of
     psychology, Vols. 1 and 2.* Cambridge, MA: Schenkman.

400. Stewart, A. J., & Platt, M. B. (Eds.). (1982). Studying
     women in a changing world. Special Issue, *Journal of Social
     Issues, 38*(1), 1-124.

401. Strouse, J. (Ed.). (1974). *Women and analysis.* New York:
     Viking.

402. Sutton-Smith, B. (1979). The play of girls. In C. B. Kopp
     (Ed.), *Becoming female: Perspectives on development* (pp.
     229-258). New York: Plenum, 1979.

403. Svejda, M. J., Campos, J. J., & Emde, R. N. (1981). Mother-
     infant "bonding": Failure to generalize. *Annual Progress in
     Child Psychiatry & Child Development,* 49-57.

404. Tangri, S. S., & Strasburg, G. L. (1979). Can research on
     women be more effective in shaping policy? *Psychology of
     Women Quarterly, 3,* 321-343.

405. Tanur, J., Mosteller, F., Kruskal, W., Link, R., Pieters, R.,
     Rising, G., & Lehmann, E. (1978). *Statistics: A guide to
     the unknown.* 2nd Ed. San Francisco: Holden-Day.
     Examines the assumptions and reasoning behind the use and
     interpretation of statistics in biology, medicine, politics,
     social interaction, sports, and daily life. Offers alternate
     hypotheses. Classic articles and compelling topics. Includes
     statistical exposure of selection bias for Benjamin Spock's
     womanless jury and documents opinion change about women
     presidents over the last 40 years.

406. Tavris, C., & Baumgartner, A. I. (1983, February). How
     would your life be different? *Redbook,* pp. 92-95.

407. Tavris, C., & Wade, C. (1984). *The longest war: Sex
     differences in perspective.* New York: Harcourt Brace
     Jovanovich.
     Misogyny, sex differences, theories of sex role socialization,
     and the world of work.

408. Terman, L. M. & Miles, C. C. (1936). *Sex and personality.* New Haven, CT: Yale University Press.

409. Terry, W. S. (1980). Tracing psychologists' "roots": A project for history and systems course. *Teaching of Psychology, 7,* 176-177.

410. Tesser, A., & Krauss, H. (1976). On validating a relationship between constructs. *Educational and Psychological Measurement, 36,* 111-121.
Suggests that obtained relationships and effects must be interpreted with reference to the theoretical constructs used to define variables.

411. Test, M. A., & Berlin, S. B. (1981). Issues of special concern to chronically mentally ill women. *Professional Psychology, 12.* 134-144.

412. Tevlin, H. E., & Leiblum, S. R. (1983). Sex-role stereotypes and female sexual dysfunction. In V. Franks & E. Rothblum (Eds.), *The stereotyping of women: Its effects on mental health.* New York: Springer.

413. The Hispanic woman in America. (1977, November). *La Luz,* Special Issue.

414. The Tampax Report. (1981). New York: Tampax Incorporated.

415. Thurer, S. (1983). Deinstitutionalization and women: Where the buck stops. *Hospital and Community Psychiatry, 34* (12), 1162-1163.

416. Tobias, S. (1986). Peer perspectives on the teaching of science. *Change, 18,* 36.

417. Turrini, P. (1980). Psychological crises in normal pregnancy. In B. Blum (Ed.), *Psychological aspects of pregnancy birthing and bonding.* Human Sciences Press, Inc. [Reprinted in J. Williams (Ed.), *Psychology of women selected readings* (2nd ed.) (pp. 391-400). New York: Norton.]

418. Unger, R. K. (1979). Toward a redefinition of sex and gender. *American Psychologist, 34,* 1085-1094.
Letters of comment in *American Psychologist, 35,* 940-941.

419. ———. (1981). Sex as a social reality: Field and laboratory research. *Psychology of Woman Quarterly, 5,* 645-653.

420. ———. (1983). Through the looking glass: No wonderland yet! (The reciprocal relationship between methodology and models of reality). *Psychology of Women Quarterly, 8,* 9-32.

421. Vance, C. E. (Ed.). (1984). *Pleasure and danger: Exploring female sexuality.* Boston: Routledge and Kegan Paul.

422. Voda, A. M., Donnerstein, M., & O'Donnell, S. R. (1982). *Changing perspectives on menopause.* Austin: University of Texas Press.

423. Voss, J., & Gannon, L. (1978). Sexism in the theory and practice of clinical psychology. *Professional Psychology, 9,* 623-632.

424. Walker, L. E. (1980). *The battered woman.* New York: Harper & Row.

425. ———. (1981). Battered women: Sex roles and clinical issues. *Professional Psychology, 12,* 81-91.

426. ———. (1984a). *The battered woman syndrome.* New York: Springer.
A comprehensive view of the circumstances, progress, and results of the battering experience.

427. ———. (1984b). Violence against women: Implications for mental health policy. In L. E. Walker (Ed.), *Women and mental health policy.* Beverly Hills, CA: Sage.

428. ———. (Ed.). (1984c). *Women and mental health policy.* Beverly Hills, CA: Sage.
In addition to containing reviews of the literature in a variety of important topic areas as indicated by separate listings on this bibliography, as a whole this book provides an excellent overview of women's issues in the mental health policy making process.

429. Walker, M., & Brodsky, S. (Eds.). (1976). *Sexual assault: The victim and the rapist.* Lexington, MA: Lexington Books.
Reviews literature, identifying and correcting myths and stereotypes about sexual assault.

430. Wallston, B. S. (1981). What are the questions in Psychology of Women? A feminist approach to research. *Psychology of Women Quarterly, 5,* 597-617.

431. Walsh, M. R. (1979). *Doctors wanted: No women need apply.* New Haven, CT: Yale University Press.

432. ――――. (1986a). Academic professional women organizing for change: The struggle in psychology. *Journal of Social Issues, 41*(4), 17-27.

433. ――――. (1986b). The psychology of women course: A continuing catalyst for change. *Teaching of Psychology, 12*(4), 198-203.

434. ――――. (1987). *Different voices: Ongoing debates in the psychology of women.* New Haven, CT: Yale University Press, in preparation.

435. Walster, E., & Walster, G. W. (1978). *A new look at love.* Reading, MA: Addison Wesley.

436. Weideger, P. (1976). *Menstruation and menopause.* New York: Knopf.
Valuable chapter on menarche and puberty rites.

437. Weintraub, M., & Brown, L. M. (1983). The development of sex-role stereotypes in children: Crushing realities. In V. Franks & F. Rothblum (Eds.), *The stereotyping of women: Its effects on mental health* (pp. 30-58). New York: Springer.

438. Weisner, T. S. (1979). Some cross-cultural perspectives on becoming female. In C. B. Kopp (Ed.), *Becoming female: Perspectives on development,* (pp. 313-332). New York: Plenum.

439. Weisstein, N. (1971). Psychology constructs the female, or the fantasy life of the male psychologist. In M. H. Garskof, (Ed.), *Roles women play: Readings toward women's liberation* (pp. 68-83). Belmont, CA: Brooks/Cole.

440. ――――. (1977). "How can a little girl like you teach a great big class of men?", the Chairman said, and other adventures of a woman in science. In Ruddick, S., & Daniels, P. (Eds.), *Working it out* (pp. 241-250). New York: Pantheon Books.

441. Weitzman, L. (1979). *Sex role socialization.* Palo Alto, CA: Mayfield Publishing.
A readable introduction to the literature on sex-role socialization, containing information about processes and consequences of sex-role socialization from infancy through college and identifying variations in socialization by class, race, and ethnicity.

442. Williams, J. H. (1987). *Psychology of women.* New York: Norton.

443. Wittig, M. A. (1985). Metatheoretical dilemmas in the psychology of gender. *American Psychologist, 40,* 800-811.

444. Wittig, M., & Petersen, A. (1979). *Sex-related differences in cognitive functioning.* San Francisco: Academic Press.
Fourteen papers by active researchers each with an extensive bibliography. Emphasis is on the biological determinants of sex differences, although sex role socialization and achievement in mathematics and sex bias in test construction are treated.

445. Wolinsky, F. D., & Wolinsky, S. R. (1981). Expecting sick-role legitimation and getting it. *Journal of Health and Social Behavior, 22,* 229-242.

446. Woolley, H. T. (1910). Psychological literature: A review of the recent literature on the psychology of sex. *Psychological Bulletin, 7,* 335-342.

447. Worell, J. (1978). Sex roles and psychological well-being: Perspectives on methodology. *Journal of Consulting and Clinical Psychology, 46,* 777-791.

448. Worell, J., & Garret-Fulks. (1983). The resocialization of single-again women. In V. Franks & E. Rothblum (Eds.), *The stereotyping of women: Its effects on mental health* (pp. 201-229). New York: Springer.

449. Wynne, J. D. (1982). *Learning statistics.* New York: Macmillan. This introductory statistics textbook incorporates a chapter on learning strategies for those without confidence in math. An appendix describes self-help progressive relaxation and test anxiety desensitization techniques. The stated goal of the book is to "enhance...confidence as learners" of those with math anxieties while providing a thorough topic treatment.

450. Yogev, S. (1982). Happiness in dual-career couples: Changing research, changing values. *Sex Roles, 8,* 593-606.

451. ———. (1983). Judging the professional woman: Changing research, changing values. *Psychology of Women Quarterly, 7,* 219-231.

452. Zaslow, M. J., & Pedersen, F.A. (1981). Sex role conflicts and the experience of childbearing. *Professional Psychology, 12,* 47-55.

453. Zussman, L., Zussman, S., Sunley, R., & Bjornson, E. (1981). Hysterectomy-oophorectomy: Recent studies and reconsideration of psychogenesis. *American Journal of Obstetrics and Gynecology, 140*(7), 725-729.